東海道新幹線開業50周年公式写真集　1964▶2014
The Official Photo Album to Commemorate the 50th Anniversary of Tokaido Shinkansen

ウェッジ

夢を実現した50年の軌跡

東海道新幹線は今年開業50周年を迎えます。

　昭和39(1964)年10月1日、東京オリンピックを目前に新幹線は「夢の超特急」から「現実の新幹線」となりました。当日午前10時、上り下りの「ひかり号」初列車が東京・新大阪両駅に定時到着した、との報が国鉄本社にもたらされました。徹夜で待機していた関係者の間に、どよめきと拍手が湧き起こったあの日の感激を忘れることはできません。

　あれから50年、新幹線は厳しい苦難の道を歩んできました。不況の到来、国鉄の収支悪化に伴う様々な難題の発生、たびたびの運賃値上げによる利用減、車両・設備の疲労、労働争議の頻発、それらによる他輸送機関に対する競争力の減退等に悩まされ続けました。一方、大阪万博の際の一千万人の大輸送完遂、「のぞみ」の登場、品川ターミナル完成等の明るい話題もありましたが、まさに山あり谷ありの半世紀の歩みでした。

　その間、昭和62(1987)年から国鉄改革によって、東海道新幹線は東海旅客鉄道株式会社(JR東海)の新幹線として再発足することになりました。これを機に、車両や設備の改良・更新を進めると共に、より多くのお客様をお迎えすべく、様々な営業キャンペーンの展開、新商品の開発等ができるようになりました。「シンデレラ・エクスプレスキャンペーン」によるイメージアップ、「そうだ　京都、行こう。」等

の観光キャンペーンも多くの話題を提供し、エクスプレス予約など新しい販売システムの導入等もありお客様の数も次第に増えてきました。

そして現在、毎日「のぞみ」「ひかり」「こだま」あわせて323本の列車を運転し、年間約1.4億人のお客様を迎えるまでに成長しました。開業以来のお客様の累計は実に55億人に及んでいます。また、最新の技術を採り入れた最高営業速度時速300kmの性能をもち、快適な車内で情報機器利用もでき、省エネ特性にも優れたN700系車両が主力車両として出揃いました。そしてこの50年間、ご乗車のお客様の死傷に至る列車事故「0」の記録を更新し続けています。

このような新幹線50年の歩みを振り返り、その記録を残し今後のさらなる発展に資するべく、JR東海では様々な関係資料のとりまとめ、記念行事、記念商品の企画、国際高速鉄道会議の開催等、様々な「50周年企画」を進めております。

この写真集刊行もそのひとつで、JR東海グループのウェッジ社によってまとめられたものであります。50年の歩みを写真で辿るものですが、次の点に重きを置いて編集されています。

第一は、新幹線の原点とも言うべき着工から開業までの経緯の紹介に重点を置いたことです。施工状況、鴨宮モデル線でのテスト走行、技術確認の模様等が詳しく紹介されています。

第二は、今日まで新幹線の安全運行を支えてきたいわば裏方とも言うべき部門の写真を揃えたことです。車両の製造、搬入、検査、修繕の様子、新幹線電気軌道総合試験車（ドクターイエロー）の詳細、車両基地、運行指令室等の運行管理部門、防災安全設備の紹介説明にも多くの写真を集めました。

もちろん新幹線列車の走行風景も収録しています。これらについては、これまでたびたび紹介されてきたものとはやや異なった角度から捉えた、よりその実態に迫るものが中心です。

このように、新幹線の運行当事者であった旧国鉄・JR東海ならではの視点に立った新しい角度から見た新幹線の写真集となっております。

この写真集を見てくださる方々が、ご自分の新幹線の乗車体験と重ね合わせてページを開いていただくと、新幹線50年の安全を支えてきた様々な努力の跡を辿り新幹線の将来に思いを馳せていただけるものと思います。

50年間に及ぶ新幹線の歴史を示すこの写真集によって、我々関係者も過去の反省の上に立ってさらなる安全・安定した新幹線を目指して一層の精進を続ける決意を新たにしているところです。東海道新幹線への永年のご愛願に感謝の気持ちを込めて、この写真集をご高覧に供する次第です。

東海旅客鉄道株式会社　相談役

須田　寬

The 50-year Path
That Made a Dream Come True

This year the Tokaido Shinkansen is celebrating its 50th anniversary.

On Oct. 1, 1964, just before the start of the Tokyo Olympics, Japan's Shinkansen (Bullet Train) changed from a "dream super express" into an actual Shinkansen. At 10 a.m., the Japan National Railways headquarters reported that the first Hikari super express trains arrived on time at both Shin-Osaka Station and Tokyo Station. Those involved who waited overnight for their arrival let out a collective sigh and applauded. It was an unforgettable moment.

It's been 50 years since that day, and the Shinkansen has traveled a harsh and difficult road. There was a recession that led to various problems JNR had to address on a continuing basis, including poor finances and frequent fare increases that caused a decrease in ridership; the wear-and-tear of rolling stock; frequent labor disputes; and competition from other forms of transportation. But there was also good news: during the Osaka Expo of 1970 the 10 millionth customer rode the Shinkansen, the Nozomi service was launched, and the Shinagawa Terminal in Tokyo was completed. It was literally a half-century of ups-and-downs.

With the privatization of the national railways in 1987, the Tokaido Shinkansen became the Shinkansen of the Central Japan Railway Company (Tokai Ryokaku Tetsudo Kabushiki Kaisha), or JR Central. Consequently, we improved and renewed our rolling stock and facilities, and came up with various new services and products to attract more customers. We developed the Cinderella Express to improve our image, as well as sightseeing campaigns like Kyoto Campaign and gradually ridership increased, partially as a function of new ticketing systems, such as EX (express) reservations.

Ridership on the Tokaido Shinkansen has increased to 140 million fares a year by operating 323 trains a day, including the Nozomi, Hikari and Kodama super express trains. Since the Shinkansen was launched, a total of 5.5 billion customers have used the system. The N700 train series features the newest technology and has become our main type of train because of its top operating speed of 300km/hour. Riders can use their communications devices in the comfort of our cars while they are in operation. The N700 series saves energy. Most importantly, for the past 50 years there have been no accidents that resulted in injury or death of passengers.

Looking back at the 50-year history of the Shinkansen we have put together a record that contributes to future generations by summarizing JR Central's documents, and we are now working on a "50th-year anniversary celebration" that includes commemorative events and products, as well as an international high-speed railway conference.

This photo collection is one of those products. As part of the JR Central group, WEDGE Incorporation put it together. The purpose is to present the accomplishments of these 50 years through photographs, which focus on the following points.

The first is an emphasis on the initial period, from the start of construction to the day the Shinkansen first opened for business, using detailed explanations about the conditions surrounding construction, test runs on Kamonomiya Test Track, and technical checks.

The second point is a series of photographs of staff working behind the scenes to maintain the Shinkansen's safety. We found many that show and explain the manufacture, transfer, inspection, and maintenance of rolling stock, as well as details about the Shinkansen High-Speed Multiple Inspection Train (Doctor Yellow), rolling stock depot, the operations departments, which contains the General Control Center, and disaster safety facilities.

Of course, we have included many photos of the Shinkansen in operation. These photos are taken from angles that are different than those that are more well-known, and include many close-ups of trains in action.

In this way, the Shinkansen photo collection was designed from a new standpoint based on the view that we of the former JNR and the present JR Central succeeded in making the Shinkansen a reality.

The people who peruse these pages will view the photos through their own individual experiences of riding the Shinkansen, tracing back through our efforts, which guaranteed 50 years of safe operations, while also thinking about the future of the Shinkansen.

By creating this photo collection of the 50-year history of the Shinkansen, we, the people who made it happen, reassert our determination to improve by reflecting on the past and aiming toward an even safer and more stable Shinkansen system. With our deepest gratitude to long-time patrons of the Tokaido Shinkansen, we hope you enjoy this book.

Advisor Central Japan Railway Company

風洞実験用に製作された木製の模型。1962.1.29
Wooden model produced for wind tunnel tests.

風洞実験の様子。東京大学
Wind tunnel tests being performed. University of Tokyo.

5分の1の模型車両を使った転走試験。1962.4.2
Trial operation using 1/5 scale model vehicle.

ブレーキ試験装置のディスクを調整する技術者。1961.11
Engineer adjusting disc brake test apparatus.

鴨宮モデル線の分岐器を通過する試験列車。1963.8.20
Test train passing switch on the Kamonomiya Test Track.

上：下り海側のロングレール上を
大阪方から上ってくる
B編成（4両）試験車両。鴨宮モデル線
top: B-model test EMU
（Electric Multiple-Unit, 4 cars）
operating in the direction of
Osaka on long rails flanking the sea.
Kamonomiya Test Track.

下：築堤を走行する試験車両。
鴨宮モデル線　1962.9
bottom: Test vehicle running on
artificial embankment.
Kamonomiya Test Track.

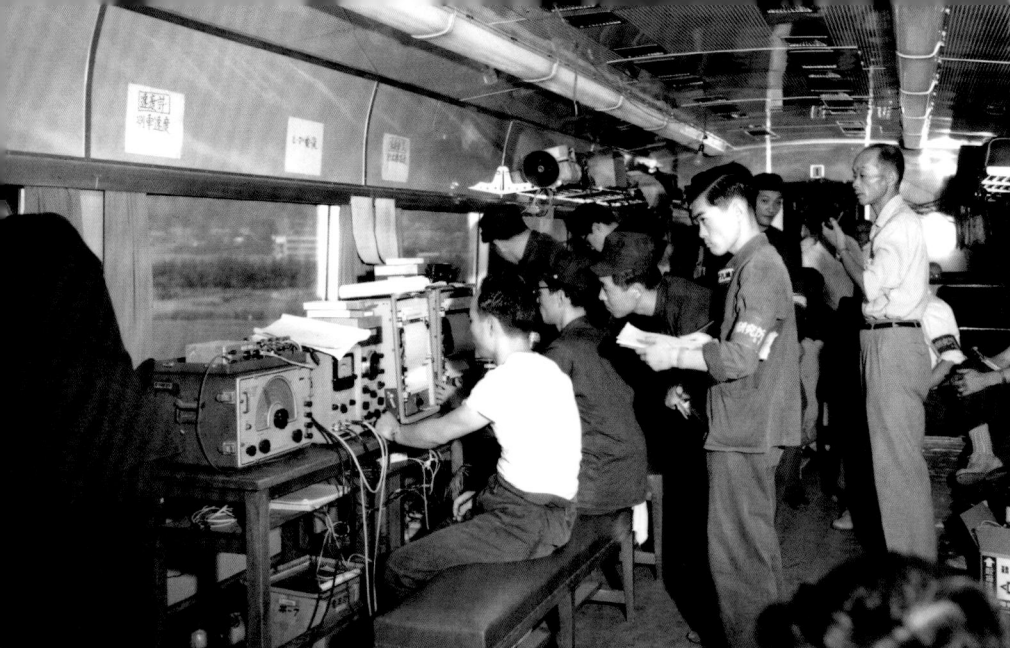

上：速度試験中の車内。鴨宮モデル線 1962.7.15
top: Inside train during speed tests. Kamonomiya Test Track.

下：A編成（2両）による速度試験。
屋根上にパンタグラフ監視用のドームが設置されている。
鴨宮モデル線　1962.9.8
bottom: Testing speed with A-model EMU (two cars).
A dome for observing the pantograph is mounted on the roof of the car.
Kamonomiya Test Track.

顔を合わせたA編成とB編成。鴨宮モデル線　1963.3.10
A-model and B-model EMUs running alongside each other.
Kamonomiya Test Track.

相模川橋梁を行くA編成。鴨宮モデル線　1963.3.10
A-model EMU running on bridge over Sagami River.
Kamonomiya Test Track.

A編成（1001＋1002）。鴨宮モデル線　1962.11.12
A-model（1001＋1002）EMU. Kamonomiya Test Track.

手前A編成（2両）とB編成（4両）の併結編成。
鴨宮モデル線　1963.7.30
A-model EMU (two cars), in front,
and B-model EMU (4 cars) running in tandem.
Kamonomiya Test Track.

A編成を使ったスラブ軌道上での新幹線用軌道試験車試験。
921-1軌道試験車が併結されている。
鴨宮モデル線　1962.7.30
Experimental track for Shinkansen
being tested with slab track and A-model EMU.
Train is connected to Type 921-1 Track Inspection Train.
Kamonomiya Test Track.

上左：苅宿トンネル付近を走行する原形姿のA編成。
鴨宮モデル線　1962.7.11
top left: Protocol design A-model EMU
running near Kariyado Tunnel.
Kamonomiya Test Track.

上右：遠景に富士山を望む。鴨宮基地　1970.3
top right: Mt. Fuji in the distance.
Kamonomiya Depot.

下：公式運転を前日に控えての試験走行。
生沢付近　鴨宮モデル線　1962.6.25
bottom: Preparation test run near Ikusawa
one day prior to official launch of operations.
Near Ikusawa. Kamonomiya Test Track.

上：鴨宮基地に留置中の921-1軌道試験車。
技術者心づくしの注連飾りをつけて。1963.1.9
top: Type 921-1 Track Inspection Train
parked at Kamonomiya Depot.
New Years ornament made by engineers is attached to the front.

下：新幹線電車救援用の911形ディーゼル機関車。
最高速度160km/h。大阪運転所　1964.11.5
bottom: Type 911 diesel locomotive
used to assist Shinkansen. Highest speed 160 km/h.
Osaka Operations Center.

上：線路上の人工雪を使った
911形ディーゼル機関車による排雪試験。
スカートに注目。浜松工場
top: Snow removal test
using Type 911 diesel locomotive
and tracks covered with artificial snow.
Note the skirt. Hamamatsu Workshop.

下：ホッパ車を改造して実施した
巻き上げ防止のための「濡れ雪化」試験。浜松工場
bottom: In order to avoid flying snow tests
are carried out with wet snow
and remodeled hopper cars.
Hamamatsu Workshop.

上：途中まで完成した上り線の相模川東側まで入線した921-1。
東京基点49キロ付近　1962.11.30
top: Type 921-1 enters the Tokyo-bound track up to
finished portion to the east of Sagami River,
about 49 km from Tokyo Station.

下：モデル線で試験を開始した
量産0系第1編成のN1編成（左）と試作B編成。鴨宮基地　1964.6.15
bottom: Tests start on model line with N-1-model EMU（left）,
first mass produced Series 0,
and test B-model EMU. Kamonomiya Depot.

上：車両メーカーで行われた量産形0系の組み立て作業。1964.2.28
top: Assembly of mass produced Series 0 in vehicle factory.

下：取り付け前の排障器のクローズアップ。1964.2.28
bottom: Closeup of pilot unit before it is attached to the train.

文字通り生まれたばかりで白く輝く0系。1964.2.28
The brand new white and gleaming Series 0.

上：整備線に搬入され、来たる営業運転開始に備える
0系量産車。大阪運転所　1964.5.21
top: Series 0 being loaded onto maintenance track
and ready to start commercial operations.
Osaka Operations Center.

下：車両メーカーで製造中の量産型0系。
窓の横に1等車を示す数字が見える。

bottom: Series 0 being made in the factory.
To the side of the window can be seen a numeral
indicating that it is a first-class car.

東京駅を発車する下り1番列車「ひかり1号」。近代日本の象徴的シーンとして国民の記憶に刻まれた。1964.10.1
The Hikari 1, first train of the day, leaves Tokyo Station for Osaka.
Japanese people remember this scene as being symbolic of Japan's modernization.

1：ブラスバンドが出迎える中、東京駅に到着した上り1番列車「こだま202号」。1964.10.1
2：大勢の人々とくす玉に見送られて名古屋駅を発車する「こだま204号」。1964.10.1
3：京都駅で工事関係者たちの「バンザイ」に迎えられる「ひかり2号」。1964.10.1
4：新大阪駅で行われた上り1番列車「ひかり2号」の出発式。1964.10.1

1 : The Kodama 202, first train of the day, arrives at Tokyo Station and is welcomed by a brass band.
2 : The Kodama 204 departs Nagoya Station as many people see it off with a celebratory streamer ball.
3 : The Hikari 3 is greeted at Kyoto Station by workers yelling "Banzai!"
4 : Departure ceremony for the Hikari 2, the first train bound for Tokyo, at Shin-Osaka Station.

1	2
3	4

1：開業を1カ月あまり後に控え、報道陣のインタビューに応える国鉄十河前総裁。1964.8.24
2：開業日の下り1番列車「ひかり1号」のサボ。開業当初は在来線と同様に手差しのものを使用していた。1964.10.1
3：乗客で賑わう開業初日の東京駅プラットホーム。1964.10.1
4：東京駅八重洲南口の新幹線切符売り場。当時はまだ手売りだった。1964.10.28

1 : One month prior to the start of regular operations, former JNR President Sogo is interviewed by the press.
2 : Sign on the Hikari 1, the first train bound for Osaka, on opening day. Manually changed signs like those used on conventional railway were initially used.
3 : The Shinkansen platform at Tokyo Station on first day of operations is crowded with passengers.
4 : Shinkansen ticket office at the Yaesu South Exit of Tokyo Station.

新幹線総合指令所。
Shinkansen General Control Center.

0系に興味津々の親子連れ。
新幹線はいつの時代も子供たちの憧れの的。
A mother and her children express interest in Series 0.
The Shinkansen has always fascinated youngsters.

霊峰富士を望みつつ駆け抜ける0系。三島〜新富士間　1965.3
Series 0 racing along with sacred Mt.Fuji in the background. Between Mishima and Shin-Fuji.

舞阪付近を走行する12両編成の0系。浜松〜豊橋間
Series 0, composed of 12 cars, running through Maisaka.
Between Hamamatsu and Toyohashi.

東海道本線に代わり、東海道新幹線が日本の大動脈となった。新横浜〜小田原間
The Tokaido Shinkansen replaces the Tokaido Main Line as Japan's main rail artery.

ネオン輝く都会の夜を行き交う東海道新幹線。東京〜新横浜間
The Tokaido Shinkansen running through the neon lights of the night city. Between Tokyo and Shin-Yokohama.

上：大井基地に勢ぞろいした0系。
top: Series 0 at Oi Depot.

下左：シートカバー交換作業。
bottom left: Changing seat covers.

下中：安全のみならずホスピタリティーも
新幹線が世界に誇るサービスのひとつ。
bottom center: Safety is the protocol,
but hospitality is also an important component of
the Shinkansen's value.

下右：全般検査を受ける0系車両。一定走行キロごとに検査を受け、
安全に万全を期す。浜松工場　1997.9.17
bottom right: Series 0 cars receiving general overhaul,
which is carried out periodically in order to ensure 100% safety.
Hamamatsu Workshop.

雪晴れの関ヶ原を行く0系。岐阜羽島〜米原間　1995.1.10
Series 0 running through sunny Sekigahara after a snowfall.
Between Gifu-Hashima and Maibara.

名古屋駅に到着した0系もうっすら雪化粧。1991.2.25
Series 0 arriving at Nagoya Station with a light accumulation of snow.

雪の古戦場、関ヶ原を行く0系。スプリンクラーの水は雪の巻き上げ防止のため。岐阜羽島〜米原間　1999.2.5
Series 0 passing through the legendary battlefield of Sekigahara in the snow.
Water sprayers prevent snow from entering the engine. Between Gifu-Hashima and Maibara.

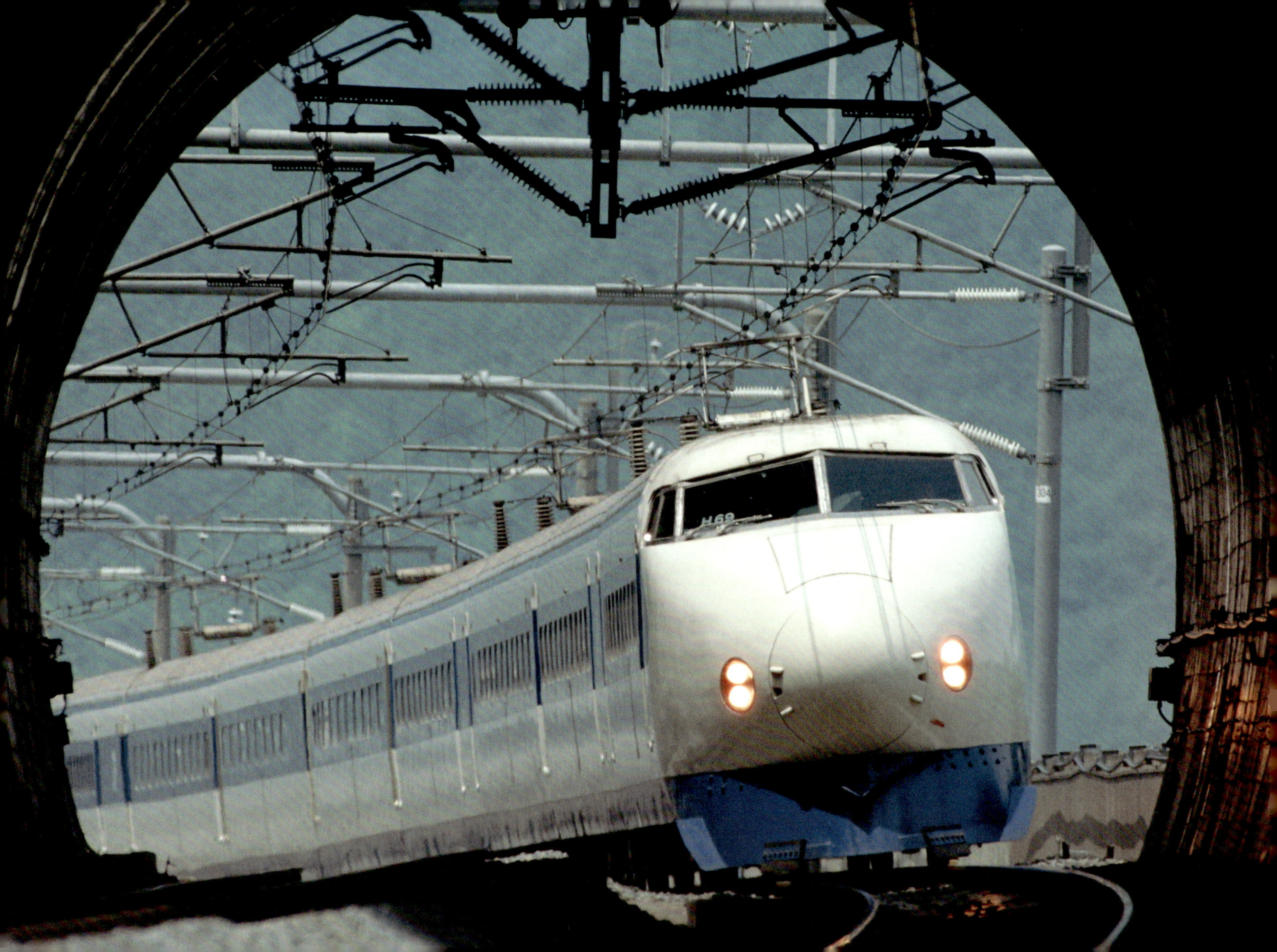
H69

ヘッドライトを光らせてトンネルに進入中の0系。
岐阜羽島〜米原間　1991.7.3
Series 0 entering a tunnel with its headlights on.
Between Gifu-Hashima and Maibara.

左：国鉄時代の0系運転室。
left: Series 0 cab during the JNR era.

上：JR東海時代の0系運転室。　1999.8.26
top: Series 0 cab during the JR Central era.

上左：真夏の緑の中を行く0系。1995.8.13
top left: Series 0 passing through green landscape in mid-summer.

上右：夕陽を浴びて走る0系。1993.3.4
top right: Series 0 against a setting sun.

下：0系「ひかり」の通過を監視する駅係員。静岡駅
bottom: Station staff watch Series 0 Hikari service as it passes by Shizuoka Station.

上：東京駅で発車を待つ０系たち。
top: Series 0 trains ready to depart Tokyo Station.

下：今はなき汐留の貨物ヤードをかすめて西へ下る０系。
この辺の風景も大きく変わった。右側の緑は浜離宮庭園。
bottom: Series 0 traveling west and passing cargo yard at Shiodome, which no longer exists. This area has greatly changed.
The green region on the right is Hamarikyu Gardens.

トンネル内ですれ違う0系。ヘッドライトが対向車両のボディを照らし出す。岐阜羽島〜米原間　1991.7.3
Two Series 0 trains passing each other in a tunnel. The headlights of one shimmer on the exterior of the other. Between Gifu-Hashima and Maibara.

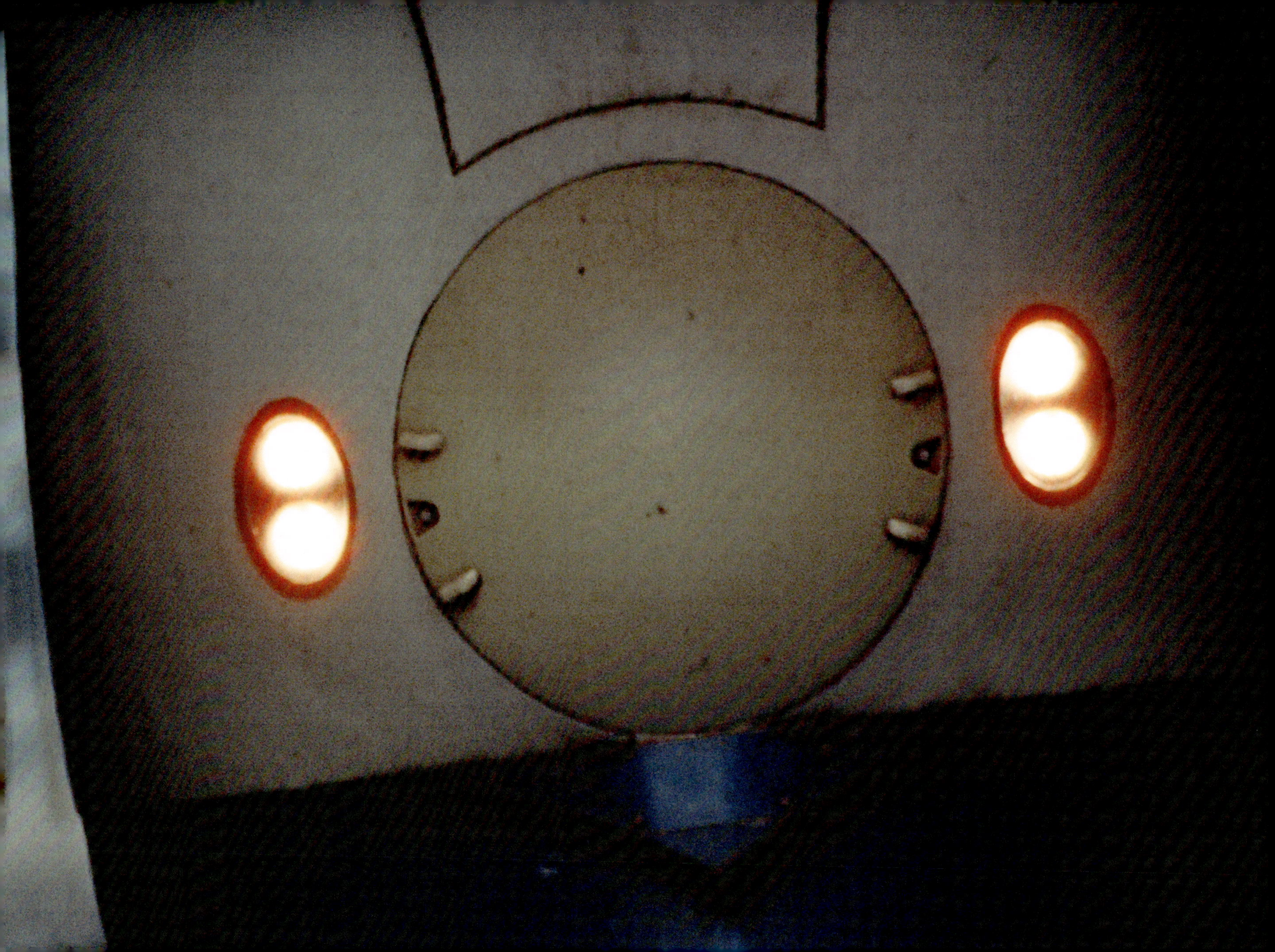

浜松工場を出る0系お召列車の編成。1966.3
Series 0 Imperial train leaving Hamamatsu Workshop.

上左：大阪運転所で待機するお召列車。
識別用マークは1966年のお召列車から採用された。1970.7.1
top left: Imperial train waiting at Osaka Operations Center.
The distinctive marking on the front was first used for
the Imperial train in 1966.

上右：多摩川を渡るお召列車。1971年8月から目印がヘッドライトの
紺色アイライン方式に変更された。1975.5.27
top right: Imperial train passing over Tama River.
The Imperial marking was changed in August 1971
to an indigo pattern around the headlights.

下：0系8両編成によるお召列車。小田原駅　1981.5.22
bottom: Series 0 Imperial train composed of 8 cars
at Odawara Station.

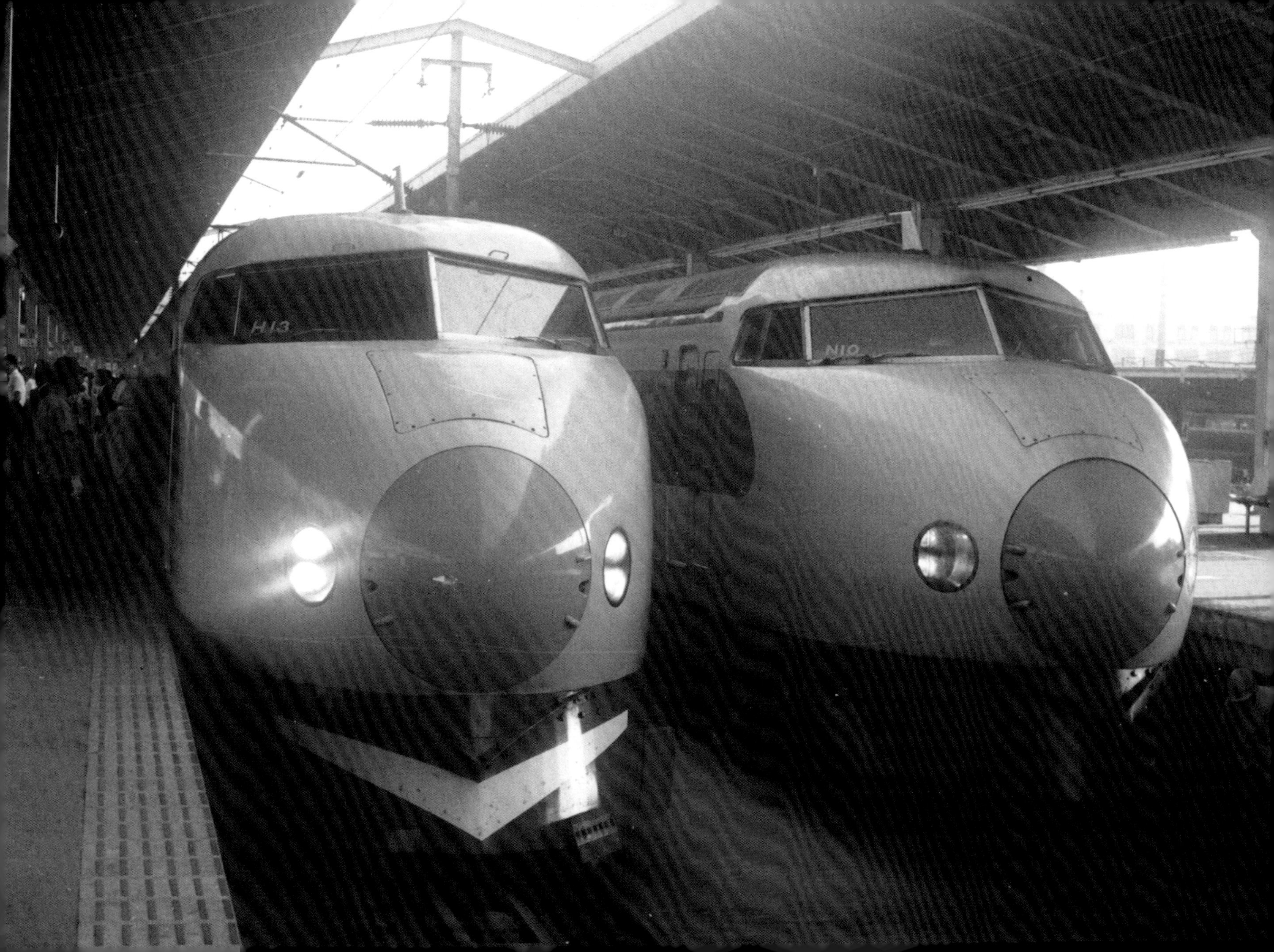
H13
N10

東京駅で発車を待つお召列車。1970.7.26
Imperial train ready to depart Tokyo Station.

上：ホーム上の点呼で敬礼するお召列車乗務員。東京駅
top: On-board train crew for Imperial train respond and salute on the platform. Tokyo Station.

下：緊張感漂う中、国鉄幹部の点呼を受ける乗務員。
お召列車乗務は今も昔も鉄道マンにとって最高の栄誉。東京駅
bottom: The atmosphere is tense while the on-board crew receives orders from a JNR official. Working on the Imperial train has always been the highest honor for a railway employee. Tokyo Station.

1：シートを一脚取り外し、テーブルを置いて足元に絨毯を敷いたお召列車の車内。飲み物を召し上がるなど休息される時のお座席。大阪運転所　1970.3.13
2：通路を挟んで反対側に設置された向かい合わせのお座席。大阪運転所　1970.7.17
3：お召列車の洗面台。特別に両陛下がお使いになるタオルが置かれた。

1 : Interior of Imperial train. One set of seats has been replaced by a table set on top of a special rug. The seats are used to rest and enjoy refreshments. Osaka Operations Center.
2 : Seats set up across from each other facing the opposite direction. Osaka Operations Center.
3 : Sink in the Imperial train. Special towels are provided for the Emperor and Empress.

東京駅を発車するお召列車。左後方に国鉄本社が見える。1966.4.15
Imperial train leaving Tokyo Station. JNR Headquarters is visible in the background on the left.

上：モノレールをアンダークロスして西へ下る
ドクターイエローT2編成。1987年の国鉄民営化後はJR東海に所属。
浜松町付近　1981.2.19
top: Dr. Yellow T2 trainset EMU
traveling west and passing under the monorail.
Following JNR privatization in 1987 it belonged to JR Central.
Near Hamamatsucho.

下：浜松町付近を走行する922形ドクターイエローT3編成。
民営化後はJR西日本に所属。1982.2
bottom: Type 922 Dr. Yellow T3 trainset EMU
running next to Hamamatsucho.
After privatization of JNR this model belonged to JR West.

有楽町付近を行くドクターイエロー T2 編成。
10日に1回程度の頻度で走る新幹線のお医者さん。
1978.10.4
Dr. Yellow T2 trainset EMU running
near Yurakucho.
The Shinkansen's physician carries out
inspections once every ten days or so.

ドクターイエロー T3編成。ドクターイエローの正式名称は新幹線電気軌道総合試験車。岐阜羽島〜米原間
Dr. Yellow T3 trainset EMU. The official name of Dr. Yellow is the Shinkansen High-Speed Multiple Inspection Train. Between Gifu-Hashima and Maibara.

上：ドクターイエローの車内。1975.11.19
top: Interior of Dr. Yellow.

下：検測機器がところ狭しと搭載されている。1996.10.7
bottom: Inspection apparatus in a tight space.

検修庫へ入線するドクターイエロー T3編成の運転台から入庫中のT2編成を見る。鳥飼基地
View of a T2 trainset already in the test garage from inside the cab of the T3 trainset Dr. Yellow EMU as it enters the garage. Torikai Depot.

車両基地にて回送列車に乗務する運転士。大井基地
Driver walks to out-of-service train. Oi Depot.

大井基地にて発車を待つ国鉄時代の100系。 1985.9.29
Series 100 during JNR era ready to depart Oi Depot.

雪の関ヶ原を走る100系。岐阜羽島〜米原間　1996.1.31
Series 100 passing through Sekigahara in the snow.

雪煙とスプリンクラーの水に赤いテールライトが滲む。岐阜羽島〜米原間　1996.1.31
Blur of red taillights seen through a mist of snow and water from sprayer. Between Gifu-Hashima and Maibara.

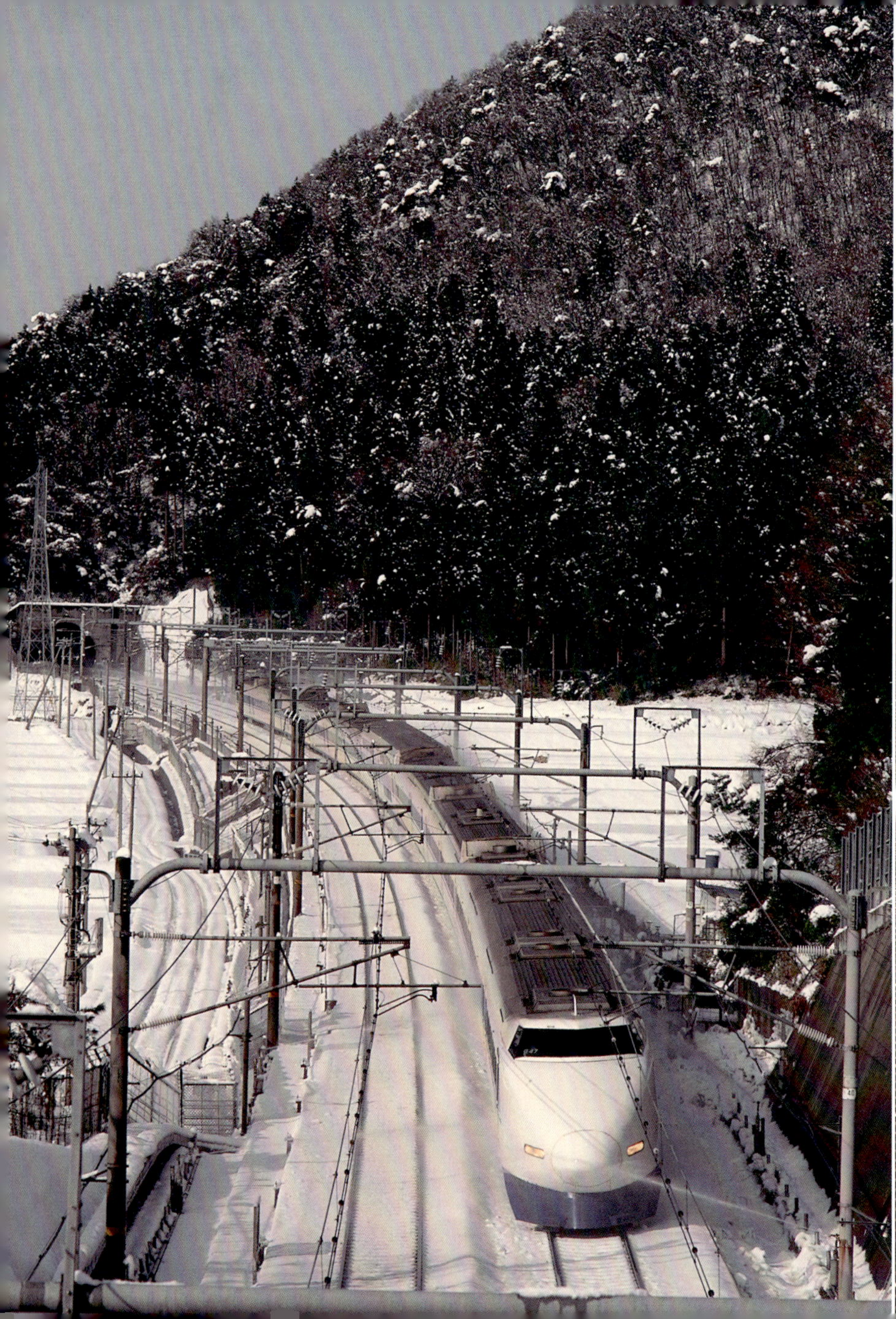

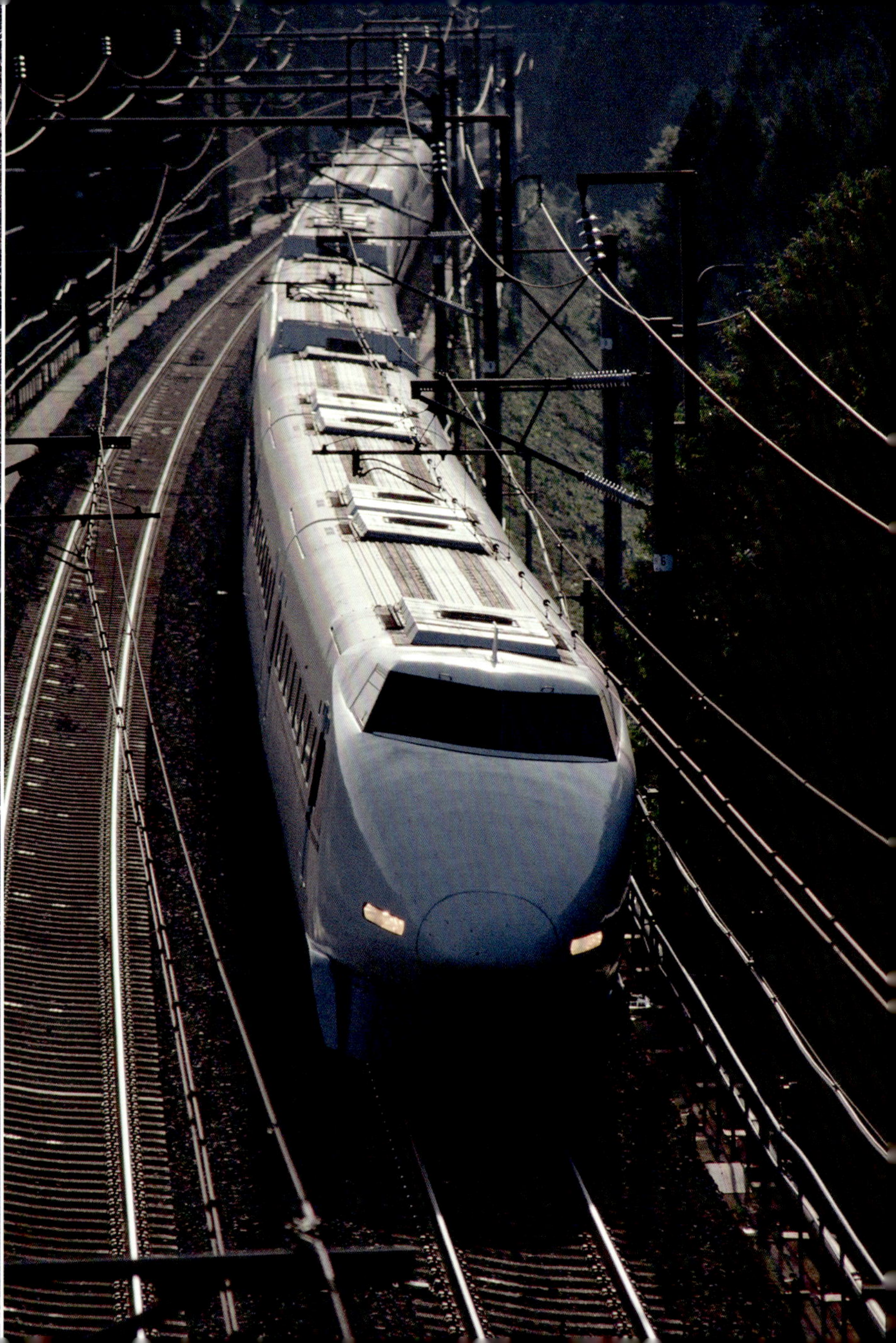

上：車体を洗浄して始発駅へ向かう。鳥飼基地
top: Train being cleaned prior to the first run of the day. Torikai Depot.

下：洗浄水が滴り落ちる。身づくろいを済ませ、これから長駆目的地を目指してひた走る。鳥飼基地
bottom: Water streaming down the train as it is washed. After being cleaned it will operate over a long distance as it heads for its destination. Torikai Depot.

左：雪晴れの関ヶ原を行く。岐阜羽島〜米原間　1995.1.16
left: Train passing through sunny Sekigahara after a snowfall. Between Gifu-Hashima and Maibara.

右：初代0系とは大きく印象が異なる先頭形状の100系。岐阜羽島〜米原間　1991.7.6
right: Frontal form of Series 100 is very different from that of the original Series 0. Between Gifu-Hashima and Maibara.

見事に晴れ上がった冬の日の朝、富士の裾野を疾駆する100系。三島〜新富士間
Series 100 running along the foot of Mt. Fuji on a beautiful winter morning.
Between Mishima and Shin-Fuji.

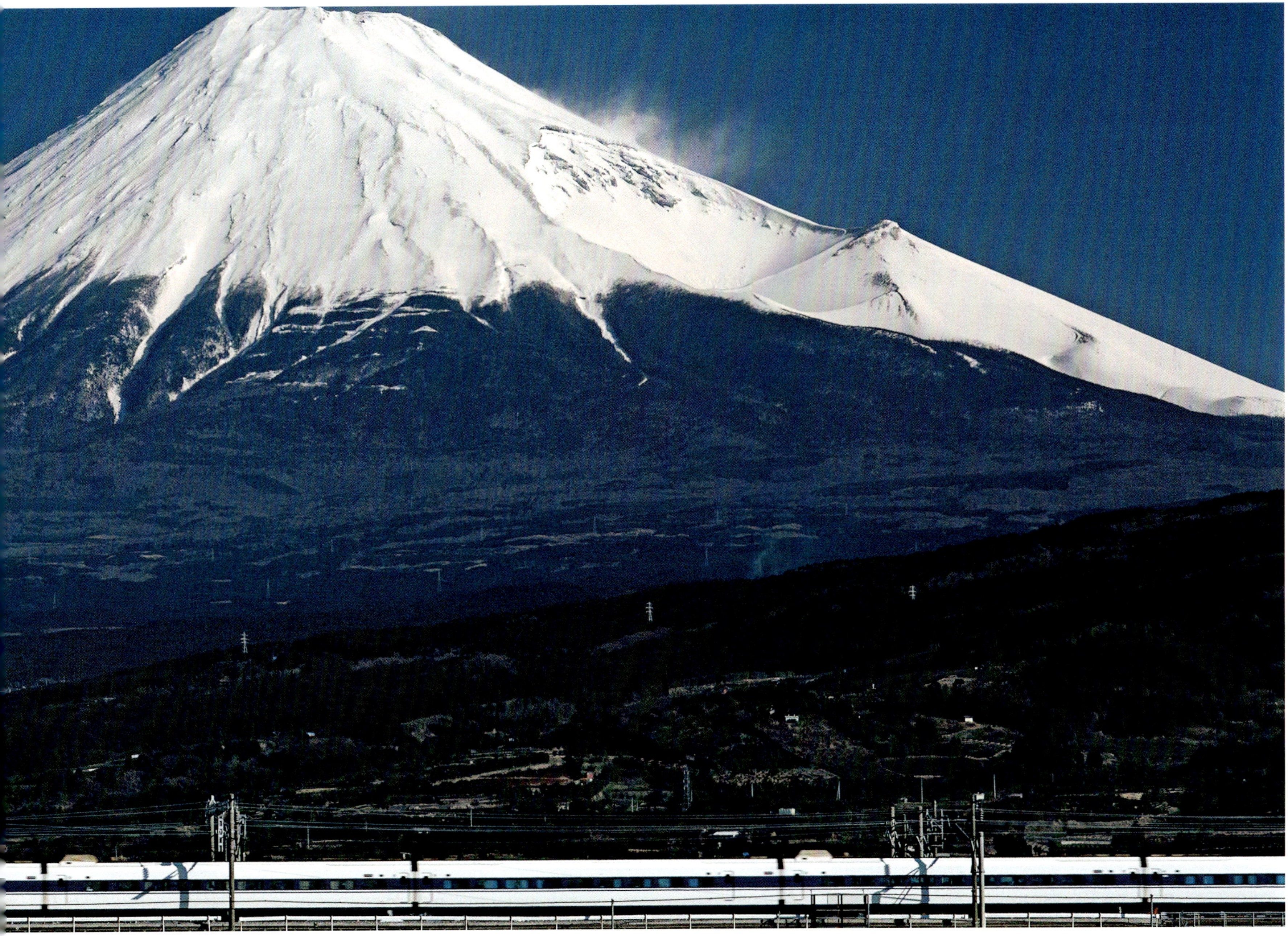

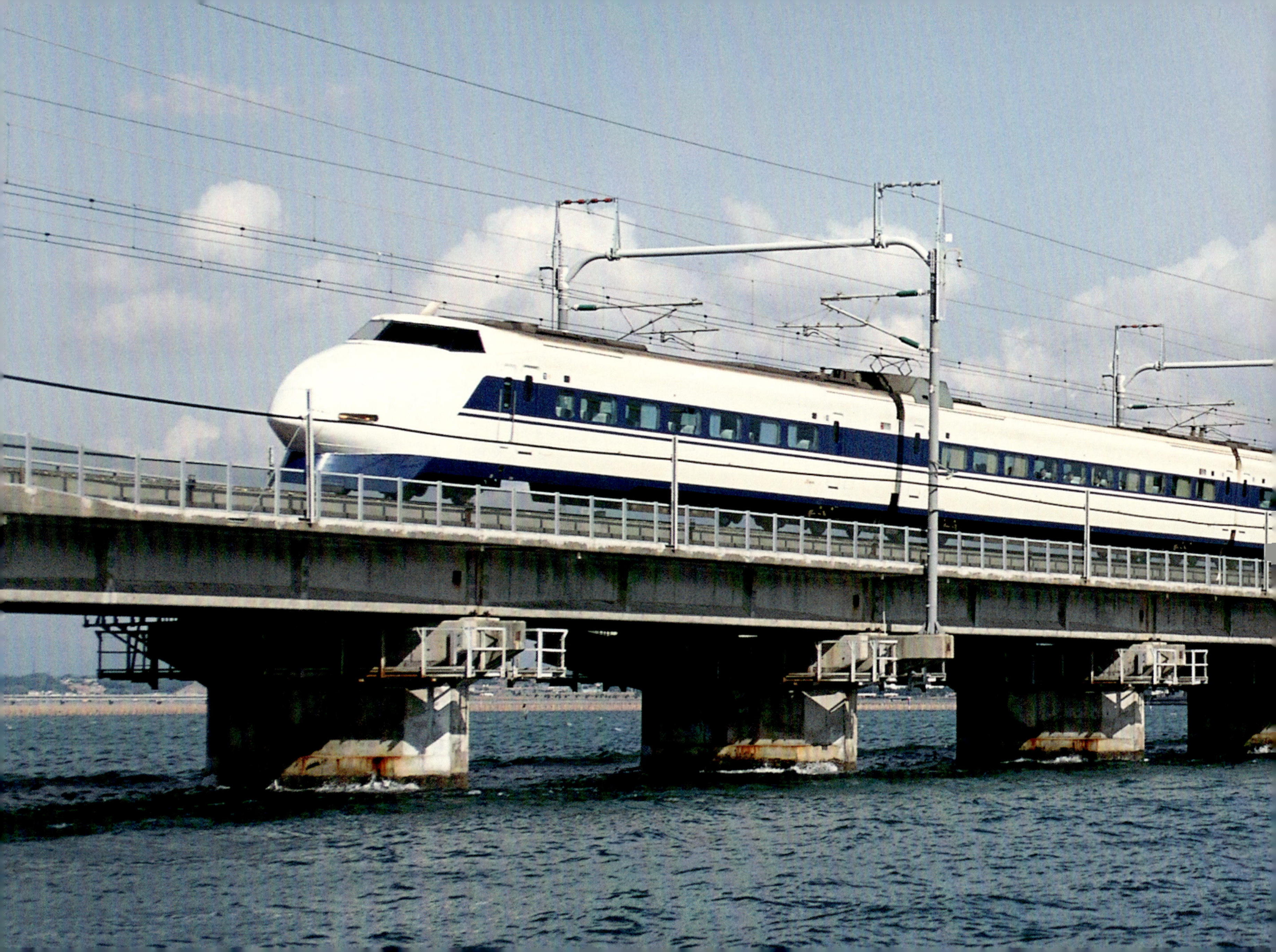

浜名湖を行く100系。東海道新幹線初の二階建車両。1998.2
Series 100 running over Lake Hamana.
The first double-decker car on the Tokaido Shinkansen.

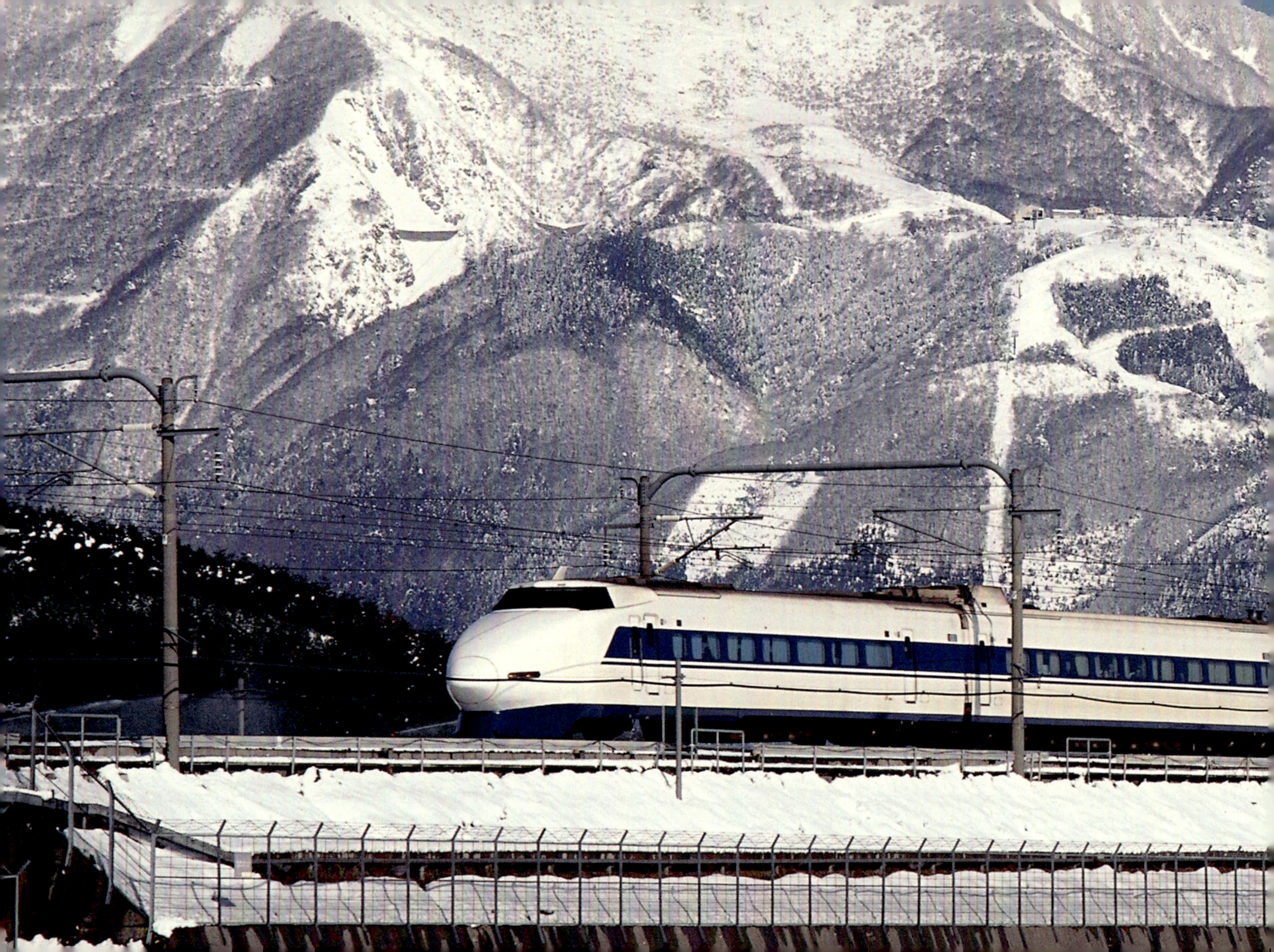

雪の伊吹山麓を行く100系。米原〜京都間　1995.1.16
Series 100 running along the foot of snow-covered Mt. Ibuki.
Between Maibara and Kyoto.

検修庫に並ぶ100系。鳥飼基地
Two Series 100 trains lined up in inspection facility.
Torikai Depot.

日々の車両メンテナンスは安全安定輸送に欠くことのできない重要な業務。大井基地
Everyday vehicle maintenance is indispensable for safe and stable operations. Oi Depot.

100系の二階建部分。国鉄時代には「New Shinkansen」の略称であるNSのマークがあしらわれていた。名古屋駅　1985.5.29
Double-decker cars on the Series 100 bearing the NS mark, which stands for New Shinkansen, during the JNR era. Nagoya Station.

トンネルの向こうから駆け抜けてくる100系。シャープなフロントマスクが印象的。岐阜羽島〜米原間　1995.11.2
Series 100 traveling through a tunnel. The sharp front mask makes a strong impression. Between Gifu-Hashima and Maibara.

伊吹山麓を走る100系。1992.9.12
Series 100 passing along the foot of Mt. Ibuki.

夏の緑濃い高架橋を行く100系。関ヶ原付近
Series 100 running along elevated track in lush green area during the summer. Near Sekigahara.

満開の桜を横目に走る。岐阜羽島〜米原間　2002.4.7
Train glances sideways at cherry trees in full bloom.
Between Gifu-Hashima and Maibara.

夕陽を浴びてひた走る100系。米原〜京都間　1993.3.4
Series 100 bathed in the rays of the setting sun. Between Maibara and Kyoto.

菜の花を見ながら。四季折々の風景が楽しめるのも東海道新幹線の魅力のひとつ。豊橋〜三河安城間　1996.4.12
Train looking down on rape blossoms. One of the attractions of the Tokaido Shinkansen is that passengers can enjoy all four seasons. Between Toyohashi and Mikawa-Anjo.

五重塔と新幹線。日本の新旧ものづくりの象徴の出会いとも言うべきシーン。京都〜新大阪間
Five-level pagoda and Shinkansen. Certainly a symbolic meeting between old and new styles of Japanese craftsmanship. Between Kyoto and Shin-Osaka.

夏の浜名湖付近を走行中の100系。東海道らしい風景。2002.7.31
Series 100 running over Lake Hamana in the summer. This scene exemplifies the Tokaido.

上：さよなら100系出発式。東京駅　2003.9.16
top: Ceremony marking the departure of
the Sayonara Series 100 at Tokyo Station.

下：100系の最終列車に出発合図を送る駅長。
「Last Run」のメモリアルステッカーが貼られた。新大阪駅　2003.9.16
bottom: The station master signals the departure of the final run of the Series 100.
The memorial decal on the side indicates the last run for the train.
Shin-Osaka Station.

100系のラストラン。100系の引退で東海道新幹線では
国鉄時代からの営業車両が全て姿を消した。東京〜新横浜間　2003.9.16
Last run of Series 100. The retirement of Series 100 trains means that
all commercial rolling stock of the Tokaido Shinkansen
of the JNR era are now gone. Between Tokyo and Shin-Yokohama

1	2	3
4	5	6

1：0系のビュフェ。 1964.7.18
2：同じく0系のビュフェ車内。開業当初はまだ食堂車はなかった。1972.7.27
3：内装が一部変更になったビュフェ。
4：0系食堂車。新幹線の食堂車デビューは開業後10年を経た博多開業前の1974年から。
5：同じく0系食堂車の内部。シートや内装にバリエーションがあった。
6：食堂車からも富士山をとの要望で通路側にも窓が設けられた。1991.12.28

1 : Series 0 buffet car.
2 : Interior of Series 0 buffet car. In the beginning there were no dining cars.
3 : Part of interior of the buffet car was changed.
4 : Series 0 dining car. The first Shinkansen dining car debuted in 1974, ten years after Shinkansen service was launched and before it reached Hakata.
5 : Inside the Series 0 dining car. There were various styles of seating and interiors.
6 : Passengers requested that they be able to see Mt. Fuji from the dining car so windows were provided along the aisle.

上：開業日の下り1番列車「ひかり1号」ビュフェ車内。満員の大盛況。1964.10.1
top: Hikari No. 1 buffet car. On the first day the buffet car was available on the train bound for Osaka it was very crowded.

下：外国人にも人気が高かった食堂車。1977.10.14
bottom: The dining car was popular among foreign passengers.

1：眺めが素晴らしい100系の二階建食堂車。
明るい陽光が差し込む車内。
2：食事をしながらの旅は
新幹線の醍醐味のひとつだった。
3：食堂車で食べる料理の味はまた格別。
4：厨房は二階建車両の一階部分にあった。
専属シェフが腕によりをかけて。

1 : The second floor dining room
on the Series 100 affords an impressive view.
Sunshine lights up the interior.
2 : Eating while traveling is one of
the pleasures offered by the Shinkansen.
3 : The taste of food in the dining room
becomes even better.
4 : The galley on the double-decker car is
located on the lower level,
where a full-time chef demonstrates
his culinary skills.

1	
---	3
2	

1：JR東海発足以降の100系にはパーサーが乗務し、よりきめの細かいサービスを提供した。東京駅
2：乗務前のパーサーはホームで整列して列車を待つ。東京駅
3：入線する300系を整列して迎えるパーサー。東京駅　1997.1.14

1 : Pursers have worked on the Series 100 ever since JR Central was established to provide even better service. Tokyo Station.
2 : Pursers lined up and waiting on the platform for the train to arrive before they start working. Tokyo Station.
3 : Pursers welcoming Series 300 as it arrives at the platform. Tokyo Station.

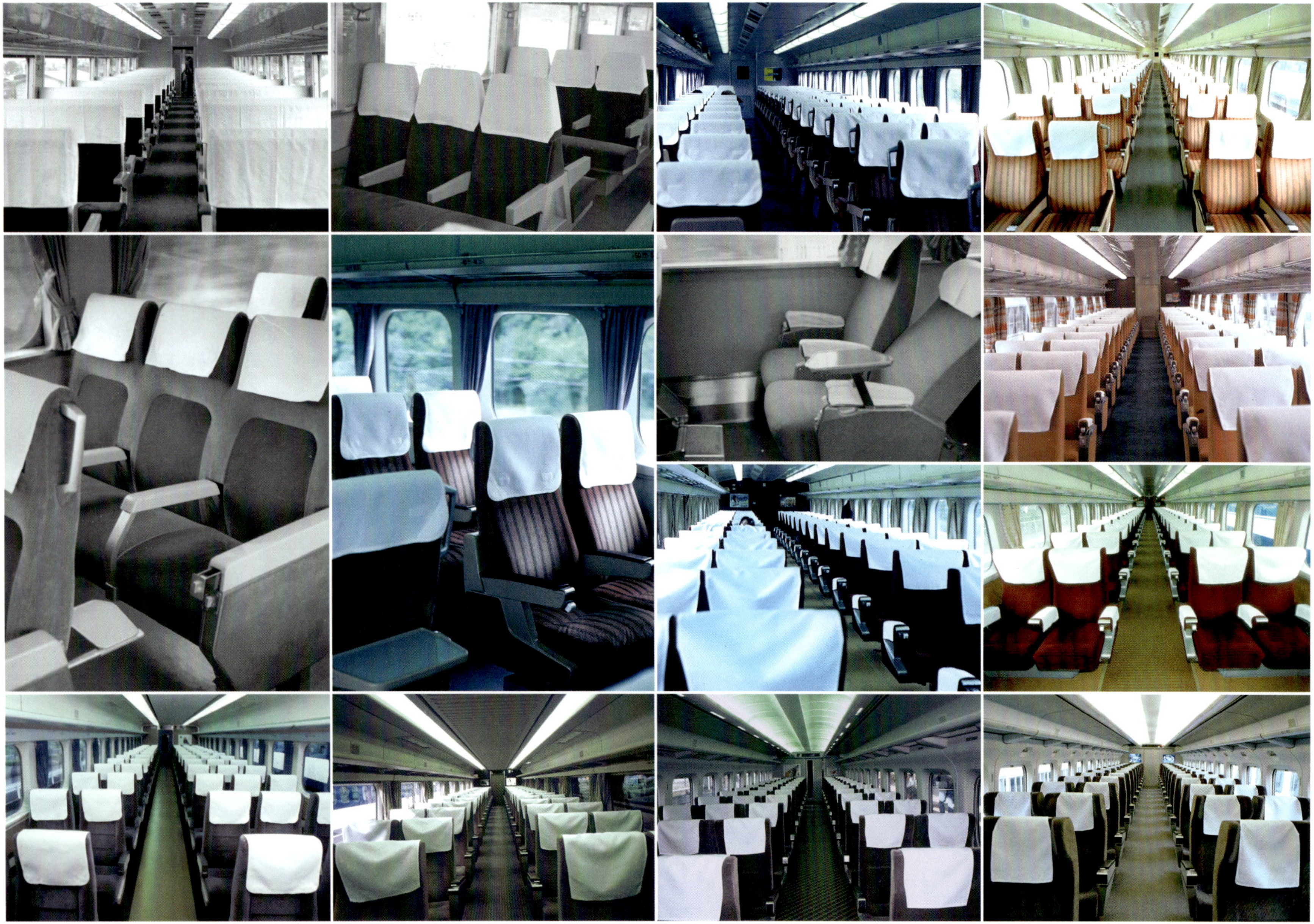

1,2：試作車両のシート。3,4,5,6：0系普通席。7,8,9,10：0系グリーン席。11：100系普通席。
12：100系グリーン席。13：300系普通席。14：300系グリーン席。15：700系普通席。
16：700系グリーン席。17：N700系普通席。18：N700系グリーン席。19：N700系グリーン席。
20：N700A普通席。21：N700Aグリーン席。22：100系1人用個室。23：100系2人用個室。
24：100系3人用個室。25：100系4人用個室。

1,2 : Seats on a prototype vehicle. 3,4,5,6 : Regular seats on Series 0. 7,8,9,10 : Green seats on Series 0. 11 : Regular seats on series 100.
12 : Green seats on Series 100. 13 : Regular seats on Series 300. 14 : Green seats on Series 300. 15 : Regular seats on Series 700.
16 : Green seats on Series 700. 17 : Regular seats on Series N700. 18 : Green seats on Series N700. 19 : Green seats on Series N700.
20 : Regular seats on N700A. 21 : Green seats on N700A. 22 : Single-person compartment on Series 100. 23 : Two-person compartment on Series 100.
24 : Three-person compartment on Series 100. 25 : Four-person compartment on Series 100.

上：300系「のぞみ号」出発式。
最高速度270km/h運転が開始され、東海道新幹線に新たなページが刻まれた。東京駅　1992.3.14
top: Ceremony to launch Series 300 Nozomi service,
which for the first time offered a maximum speed of 270 km/h.
A new page in the story of the Tokaido Shinkansen was turned. Tokyo Station.

下：菜の花畑を行く。300系はJR東海発足後にデビューした初の新型車両。豊橋～三河安城間　2004.3.19
bottom: Passing through a field of rape blossoms.
Series 300 is the first new train model to debut following the establishment of JR Central.
Between Toyohashi and Mikawa-Anjo.

東京駅に到着した300系と発車を待つ0系。1993.2.24
Series 300 arriving at Tokyo Station as 0 Series train waits to depart.

300系中心のダイヤに変わっても、富士山と新幹線の名コンビは変わらず。三島〜新富士間　2002.11.23
Even after the timetable was changed to accommodate Series 300, the Shinkansen's relationship with Mt. Fuji did not change. Between Mishima and Shin-Fuji

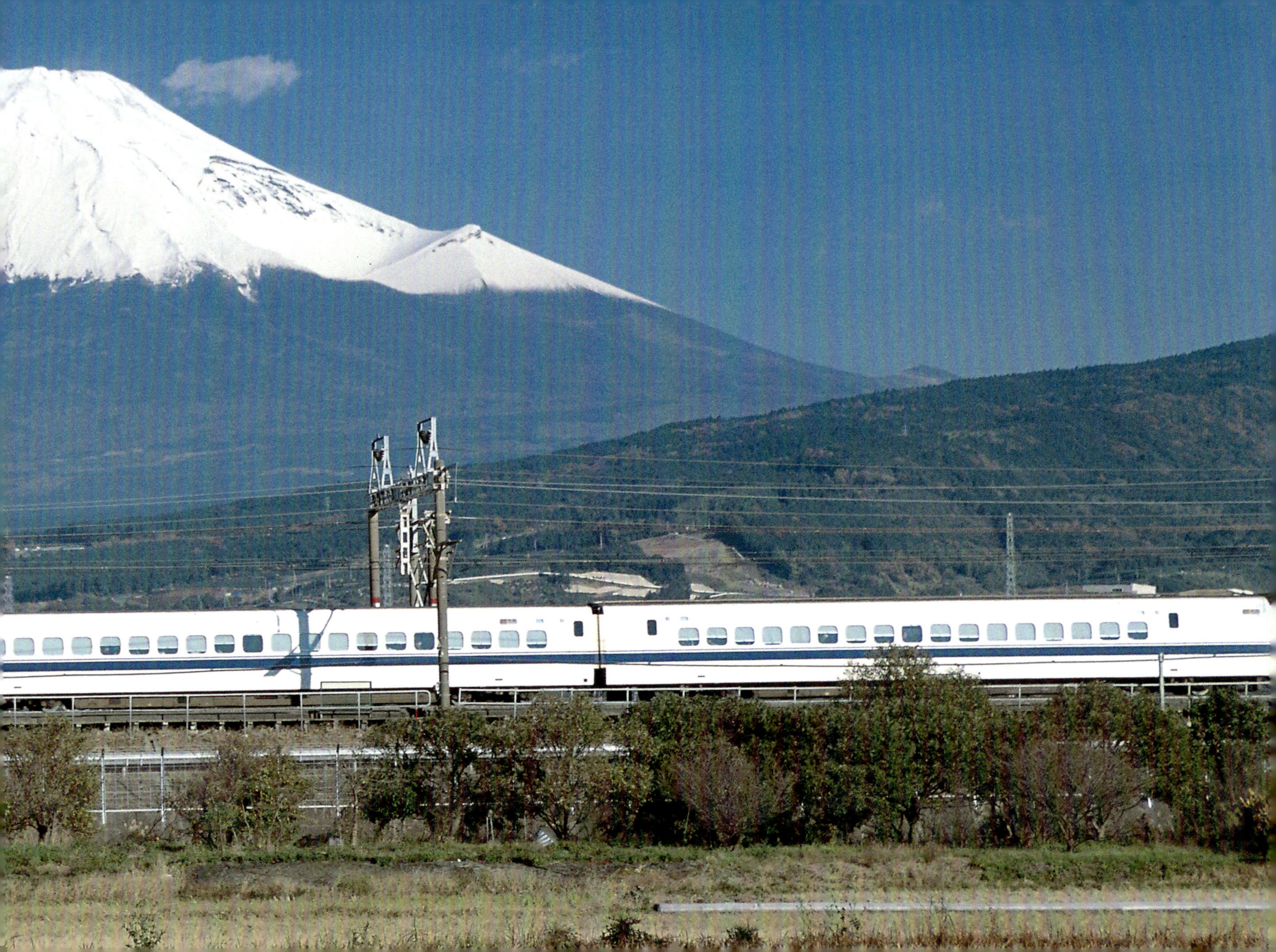

浜名湖付近で0系とすれ違う300系。0系は更新されたタイプで新設されたパンタグラフカバーとこだま2&2シートのステッカー表示が見える。1998.2
Near Lake Hamana the Series 300 passes Series 0, which had been redesigned with a pantograph cover and a decal indicating Kodama 2+2 seating.

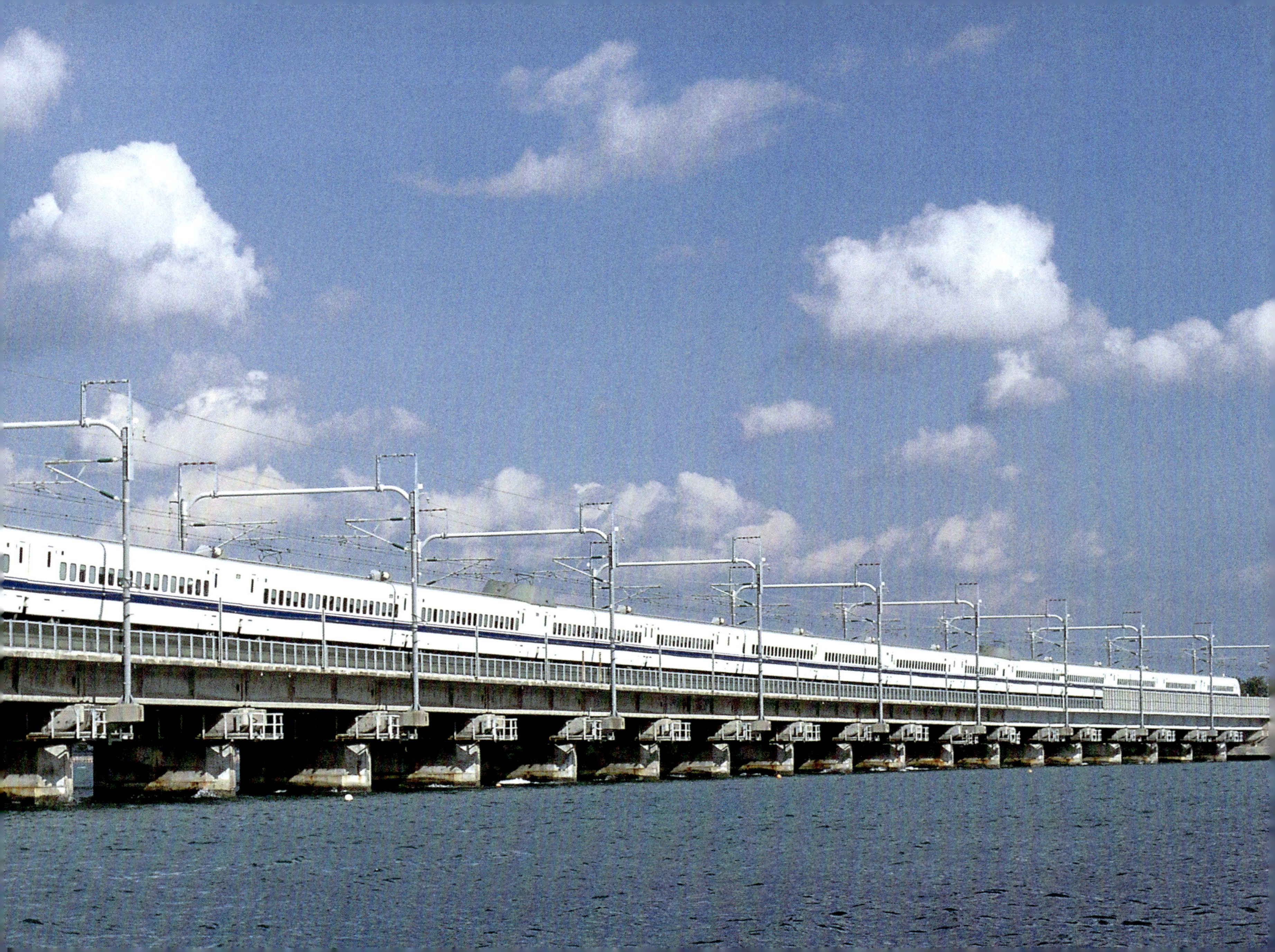

米原駅に到着した300系。2008.2.14
Series 300 arriving at Maibara Station.

300系「のぞみ」通過。浜松駅　1992.11.5
Series 300 Nozomi service passing Hamamatsu Station

左：車体洗浄機を通る300系。大井基地　1995.6.22
left: Series 300 passing through washing equipment. Oi Depot

右：全般検査中の300系。浜松工場　2006.2.21
right: Series 300 undergoing general overhaul. Hamamatsu Workshop.

大型クレーンで吊り上げられ台車を外された300系。車体の検査にも万全を期す。
浜松工場　1994.1.26
Series 300 without a bogie being lifted by crane in order to carry out thorough inspection of the train body. Hamamatsu Workshop.

名古屋のランドマーク、JRセントラルタワーズと300系。名古屋駅　1999.7.8
Series 300 and JR Central Towers, a Nagoya landmark. Nagoya Station.

上：春の伊吹山を望みつつ。岐阜羽島〜米原間　2011.4.14
top: Train looking at Mt. Ibuki in the spring.
Between Gifu-Hashima and Maibara.

下：田植えの終わった田んぼの脇を行く。岐阜羽島〜米原間　2008.5.15
bottom: Skirting rice paddies
where seedlings have just been planted.
Between Gifu-Hashima and Maibara.

冬間近の関ヶ原。米原〜京都間　2008.12.3
Sekigahara in early winter. Between Maibara and Kyoto.

車両基地でしばしの休息。大井基地
Idle trains at Oi Depot.

盛夏の伊吹山を駆け抜ける300系。岐阜羽島〜米原間　2001.8.24
Series 300 runs past Mt. Ibuki in mid-summer. Between Gifu-Hashima and Maibara.

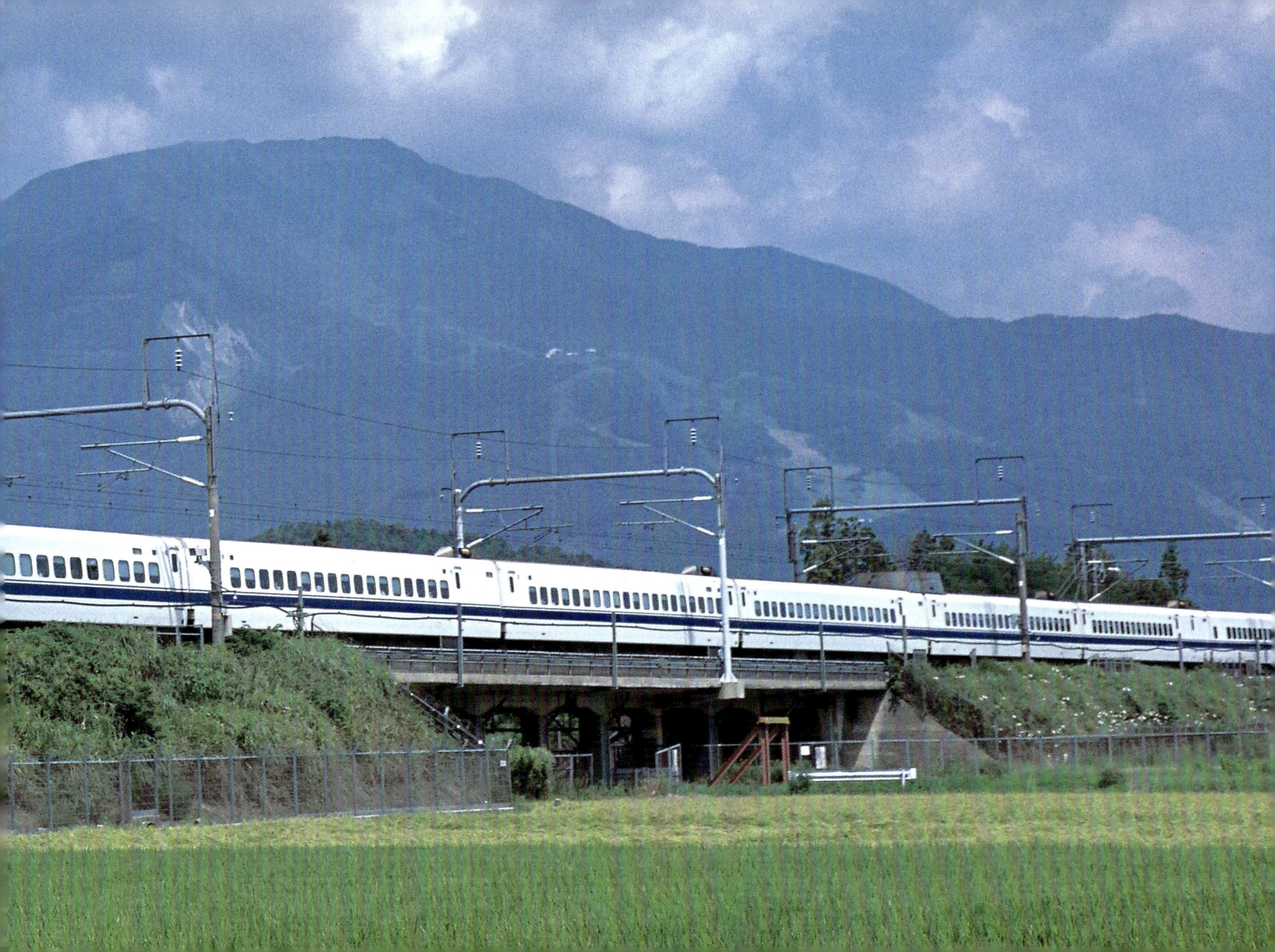

300Xは300系に続く次世代新幹線の技術開発用の高速試験車両。ラウンドウェッジ型の先頭車両。静岡〜掛川間 2000.3.1
The 300X was a high-speed experimental train created during the development of the next generation Shinkansen after Series 300. The front car has a rounded wedge shape. Between Shizuoka and Kakegawa.

丸子橋付近を行く300X。こちらの先頭形状はカスプ型と呼ばれた。
大型のパンタグラフカバーが印象的。　東京〜新横浜間　2000.9.25
300X passing near Marukobashi.
The shape of the front car is called a "cusp."
The large pantograph cover makes a striking impression.
Between Tokyo and Shin-Yokohama.

橋梁を行く300X。試験で得られた各種の貴重なデータは700系に活かされた。豊橋〜三河安城間
300X running over a bridge. Important data obtained during these test runs were useful for the development of the Series 700 Shinkansen. Between Toyohashi and Mikawa-Anjo.

ドクターイエロー T2編成と並んだ300X。先頭形状がかなり小型化されているのが分かる。　大井基地　1999.10.21
The 300X sits alongside a Dr. Yellow T2 trainset EMU. The forward shape of the first car has been reduced. Oi Depot.

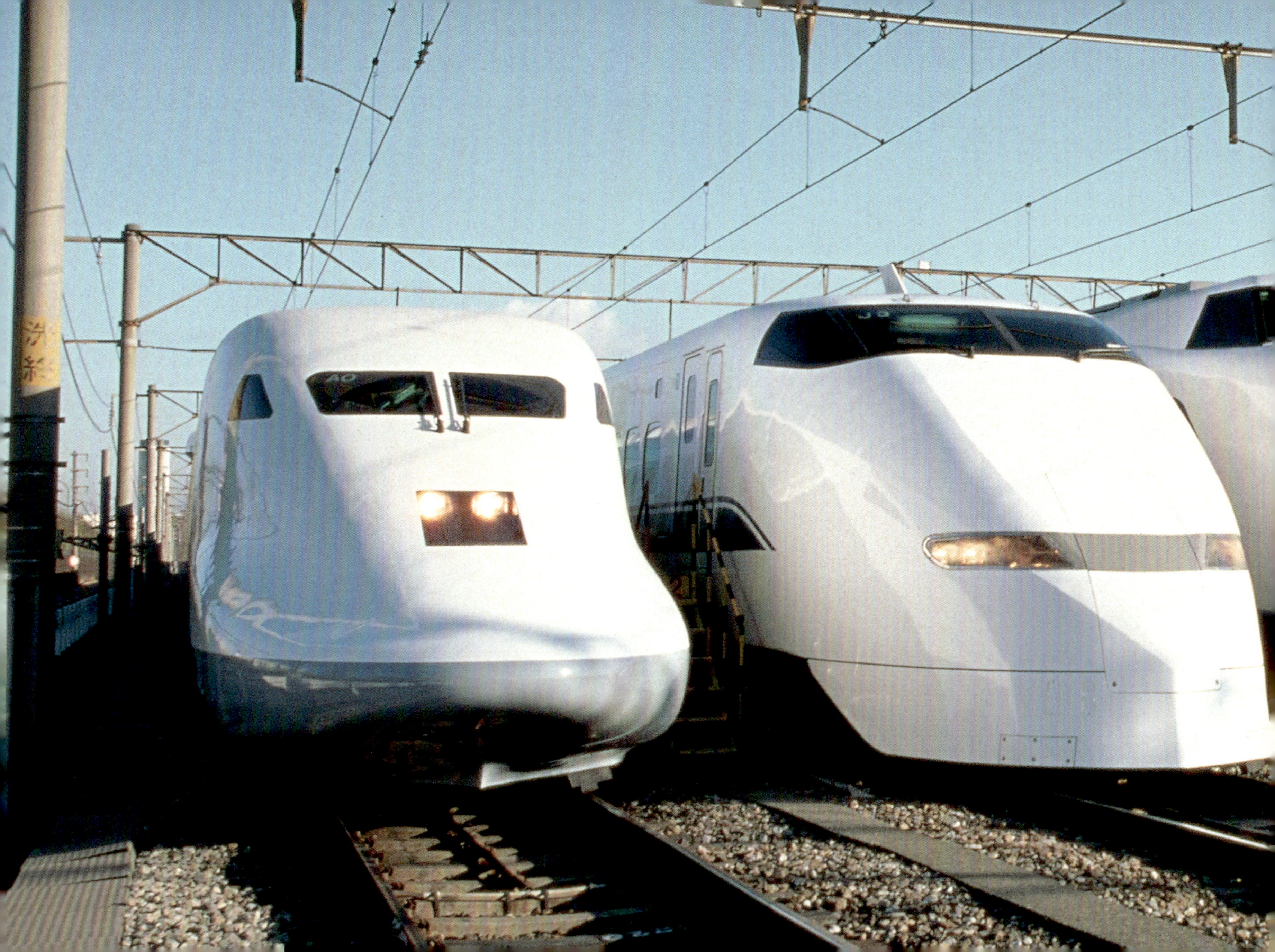

先輩車両たちと肩を並べた300X。
歴代車両の先頭形状の変化が興味深い。
大井基地
300X alongside earlier models.
Note the changes in styles of
the front cars. Oi Depot.

300系ラストランの出発式。
多くのファンとN700系の見送りを受けて。
東京駅　2012.3.16
Ceremony to launch last run of Series 300.
Many train enthusiasts, as well as the new Series 700,
see the train off. Tokyo Station.

ラストランに際して、先頭車両には「ありがとう。」の装飾が施された。
東京〜品川間　2012.3.10
On its last run the Series 300 had "Thank you" written on its front car.
Between Tokyo and Shinagawa.

上：仮台車を履いて、日本車輌から浜松工場に搬入される700系車両。
1998.12.24
top: Using a makeshift bogie, a Series 700 car is transported from Nippon Sharyo to the Hamamatsu Workshop.

下：700系新幹線電車量産編成完成式典。700系のデビューで
また新たな時代へ。浜松工場　1998.12.22
bottom: Ceremony to commemorate the completion of
the Series 700 mass-production trainset.
JR Central enters another new era with the debut of Series 700.
Hamamatsu Workshop.

「AMBITIOUS JAPAN!」の大型ステッカーを貼って走る700系。
TOKIOが歌った曲のヒットも相まって大きな反響を呼んだ。有楽町付近
Series 700 running with a large decal on its side reading "AMBITIOUS JAPAN!",
which caused much excitement since it was also the title
of a contemporary hit song by the boy band TOKIO. Near Yurakucho.

399

伊吹山麓のカーブを行く700系。
米原〜京都間　2007.5.11
Series 700 running along curved track
at the foot of Mt. Ibuki.
Between Maibara and Kyoto.

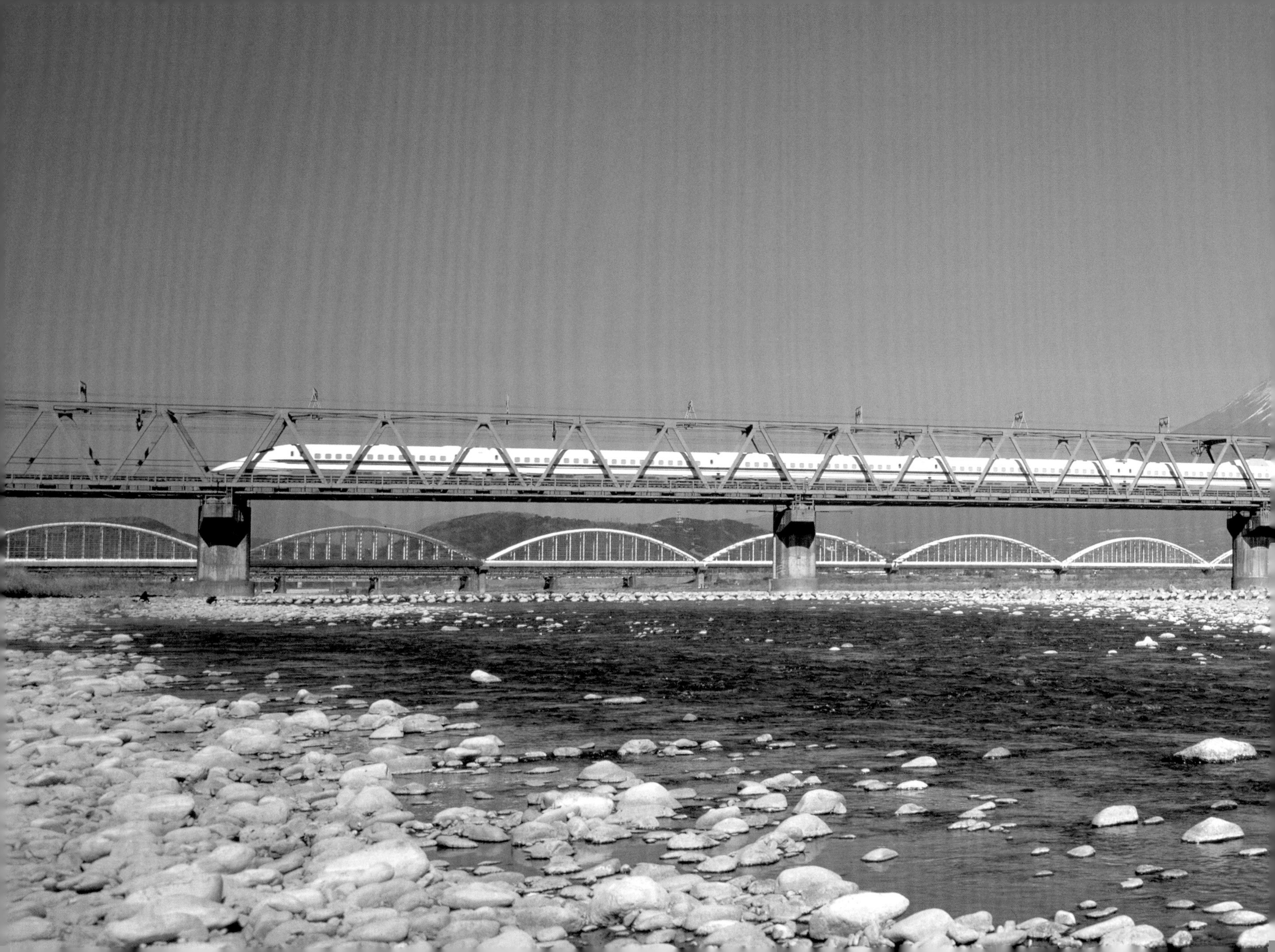

遠く富士山を望みつつ、富士川橋梁を渡る700系。1999.2.5
With Mt. Fuji in the background,
Series 700 runs on a bridge over the Fuji River.

雪化粧した木々の下を走る700系。
関ヶ原　2008.2
Series 700 running under trees laden with snow. Sekigahara.

スプリンクラーの水しぶきに包まれて。米原駅
Passing through a spray of water. Maibara Station.

建設中の東海道新幹線品川駅。2001.9.5
The Tokaido Shinkansen Shinagawa Station under construction.

建設中の品川駅仮上り本線切換工事区間を走る
電気軌道総合試験車。2000.10.15
Bound for Tokyo on a section of
makeshift track through Shinagawa Station,
where new route tracks are under construction.
Multiple-Inspection Train.

建設中の品川駅仮上り本線の切換工事区間を
300系が行く。2000.10.15
Series 300 running on makeshift track
through Shinagawa Station,
where new route tracks are under construction.

上：東海道新幹線品川駅開業記念出発式。
品川駅　2003.10.1
top: Ceremony to mark the opening of
the Tokaido Shinkansen Shinagawa Station.
Shinagawa Station.

下：東海道新幹線開業40周年出発式。
新大阪駅　2004.10.1
Bottom: Ceremony to mark the 40th anniversary of
the Tokaido Shinkansen. Shin-Osaka Station.

浜名湖畔の椰子並木を走る923形T4編成ドクターイエロー。2001.4.17
923 Dr. Yellow T4 trainset EMU running alongside palm trees at Lake Hamana.

T2編成の老朽化や300系以降の車両統一に伴い、270km/h走行を可能とするため700系をベースに2000年に開発されたT4編成。浜松〜豊橋間　2003.8.18
The T4 trainset EMU newly developed in 2000 based on the Series 700 to reach 270km/h,
following the unification of rolling stock to Series 300 and newer series and as the T2 trainset EMU was aging. Between Hamamatsu and Toyohashi.

東京駅をあとにシーサス分岐器を渡って、長駆博多までの検測に出るドクターイエロー。東京駅 2001.2.2
Dr. Yellow leaving Tokyo Station and passing over a double cross turnout on the long inspection journey to Hakata. Tokyo Station.

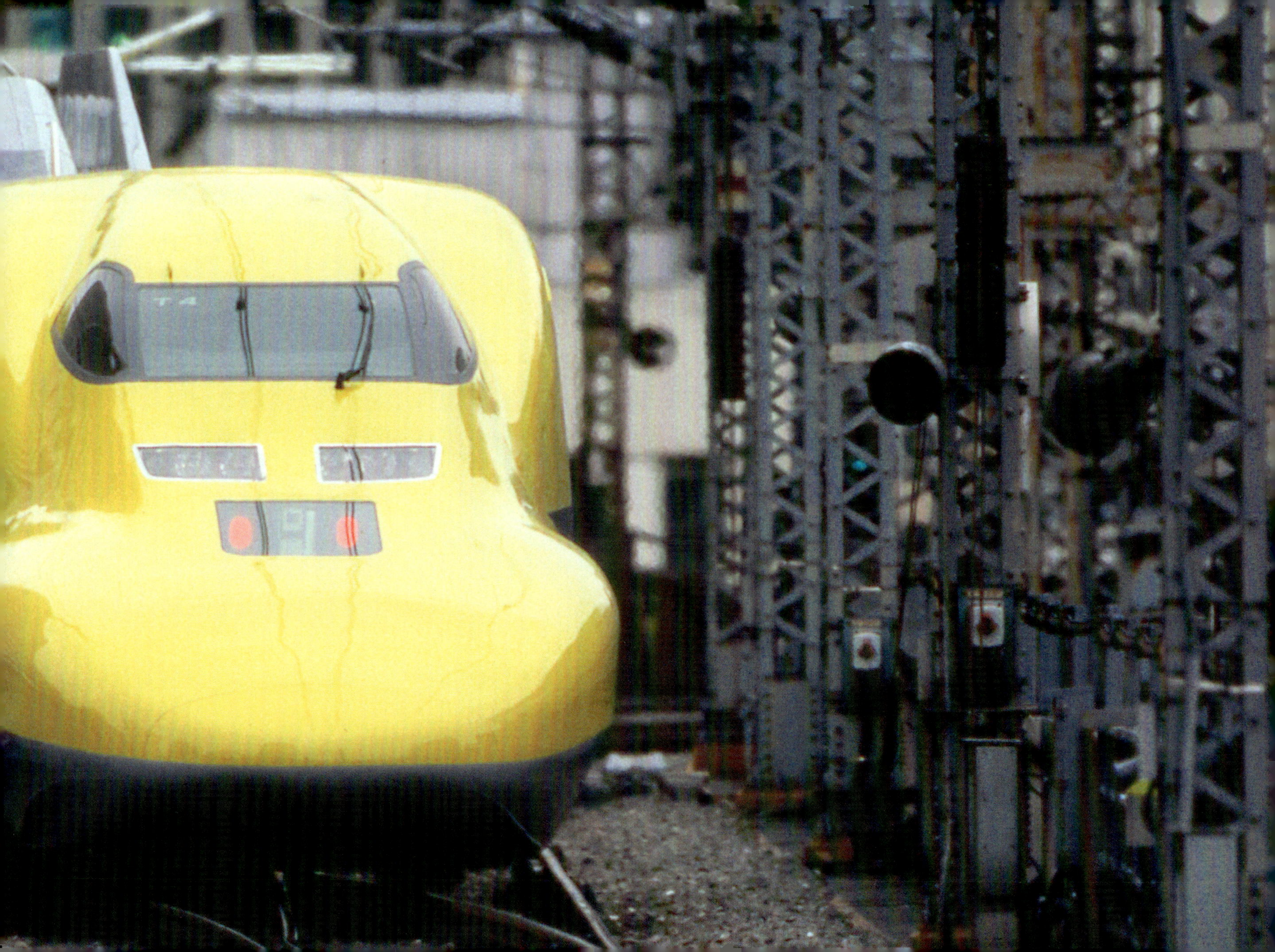

1	2
3	4

1：併結訓練のため、フロントカバーを外される700系。日比津基地　2002.10.24
2：新幹線総合事故復旧訓練の様子。日比津基地　2002.10.24
3：乗客の救護、誘導訓練。日比津基地　2002.10.24
4：パンタグラフの点検訓練。日比津基地　2002.10.24

1 : Multiple operations drills to remove the front cover of the 700 series. Hibitsu Depot.
2 : Simulation training for aftermath of a Shinkansen accident. Hibitsu Depot.
3 : Simulation training for passenger rescue and instruction. Hibitsu Depot.
4 : Training for inspection of pantograph. Hibitsu Depot.

併結される700系と300系。併結の際はATCを切って手信号で誘導する。 日比津基地　2002.10.24
Series 700 and Series 300 trains connected in tandem for simulation training.
ATC is directed to be turned off when connecting the trains by means of hand signals. Hibitsu Depot.

上：最終列車通過後の深夜に行われる、道床交換作業の様子。
列車の振動などで細かくなったバラストは定期的に交換される。
2013.3.3
top: After the final train of the day passes, the ballast is replaced.
Vibration of train causes ballast to become smaller,
so it is regularly replaced.

下：パンタグラフとの摩擦で摩耗した架線の張り替え作業。
2013.2.22
bottom: Replacing overhead cables,
which becomes worn due to friction of pantograph.

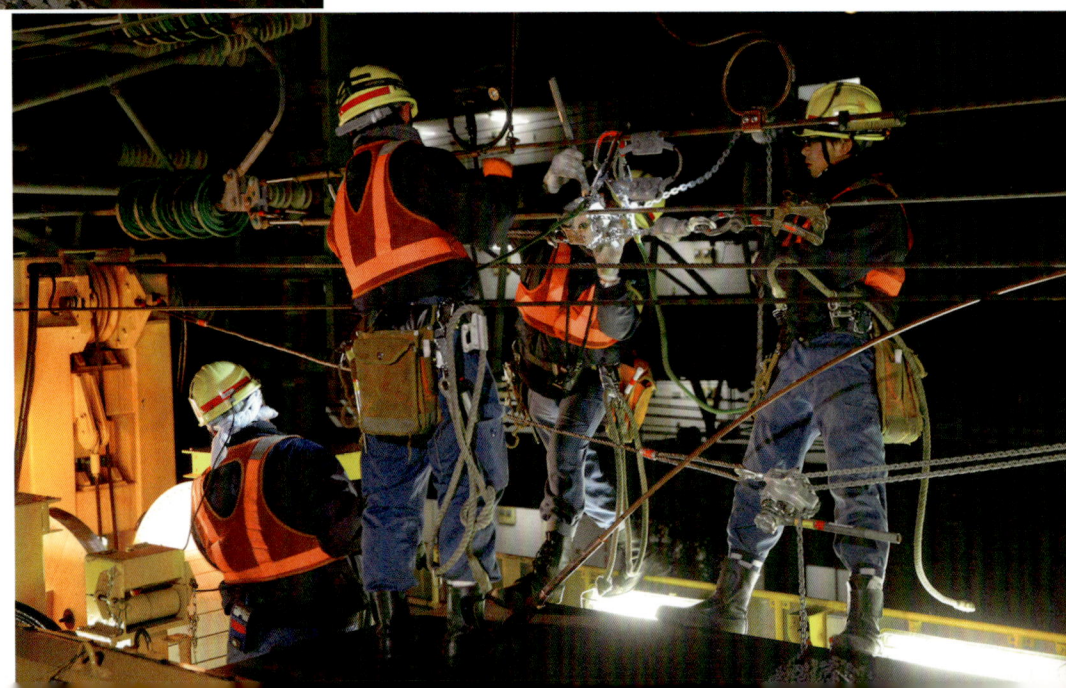

専用の保守作業車マルチプルタイタンパーを使っての道床突き固め作業。2013.3.3
Packing the ballast with the help of multiple titan bars and a specialized maintenance vehicle.

1	3
2	

1：製造中のN700系先頭車両。700系から導入されたアルミニウム合金製の中空押出型材による
ダブルスキン構造を採用している。日立笠戸工場　2004.11.29
2：N700系先頭車の構体を内部から見る。日立笠戸工場　2004.11.29
3：普段見ることのない連結器。
カバーを外すと精悍なN700系もどこかユーモラスな表情に。浜松工場　2005.3.15

1 : Front car of Series N700 being manufactured.
The double skin structure made by means of aluminum alloy hollow extrusion was
first used with the Series 700. Hitachi Kasado Factory.
2 : Interior structural view of Series N700 front car. Hitachi Kasado Factory
3 : The coupler is usually not visible.
When the cover is removed from the angular Series N700 it has a comical appearance.
Hamamatsu Workshop.

空力特性を極限まで突き詰めた、微妙な曲線の組合わせで構成される先頭形状。日立笠戸工場　2004.11.29
The best possible aerodynamic performance. The shape of the train front is a combination of precision curves. Hitachi Kasado Factory.

製造中のN700系運転席を内側から。曲線が多用されていることが見て取れる。
日立笠戸工場　2004.11.29
View from the interior of a Series N700 cab as it is being manufactured.
Many curved lines are used. Hitachi Kasado Factory.

営業列車のN700系運転席。 2007.5.23
In the cab of a Series N700 during regular operation.

1	2
3	4

1：N700系量産車に取り付けられる台車。日本車輌豊川製作所　2007.3.16
2：台車の取り付け作業。日本車輌豊川製作所　2007.3.16
3：床下側から見た台車の取り付け位置。日本車輌豊川製作所　2007.3.16
4：作業員が手で押して所定の位置まで移動する。日本車輌豊川製作所　2007.3.16

1 : The bogie of a Series N700 mass-produced car. Nippon Sharyo Toyokawa Plant.
2 : Attaching the bogie to a Series N700 car. Nippon Sharyo Toyokawa Plant.
3 : View from below of a bogie being attached to a car. Nippon Sharyo Toyokawa Plant.
4 : Workers pushing a bogie by hand into the right position for attachment. Nippon Sharyo Toyokawa Plant.

組み立てが完了し、車両基地への搬入を待つN700系。一般道を牽引されるため、
事故防止用の赤色LEDランプが巻きつけられる。日本車輌豊川製作所　2007.3.16
Assembly is complete. Series N700 is now ready to be transported to a depot.
Because it will be towed on surface roads, it is wrapped in red LED lines to prevent accidents.
Nippon Sharyo Toyokawa Plant

上：一般道路を陸送中のN700系。陸送作業は交通量の少ない深夜に慎重を期して行われる。2007.3.16
top: In order to ensure safety,
the Series N700 is transported on regular surface roads during the middle of the night, when there is a minimum of traffic.

下：新幹線車両が踏切を渡るという珍しいシーン。2007.3.16
bottom: It's unusual to see a Shinkansen itself
crossing railroad tracks.

搬入され、編成組成を終えた新製車両。浜松工場 2005.3.4
Newly manufactured cars are coupled together after being placed on the tracks. Hamamatsu Workshop.

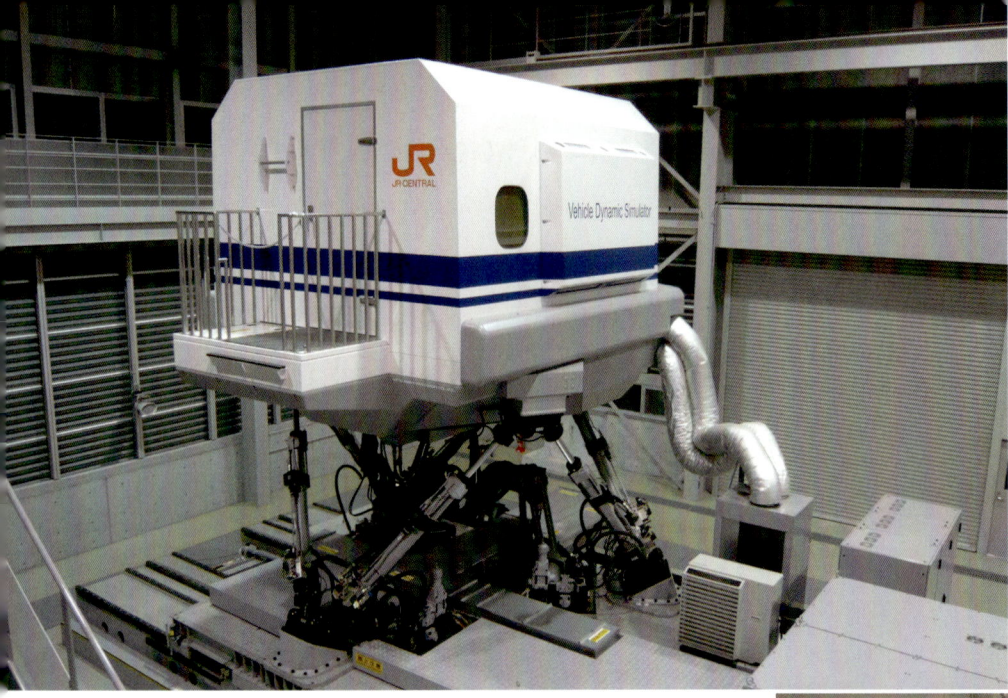

上：車両運動総合シミュレーター。小牧研究施設
top: Vehicle Dynamic Simulator. Komaki Research Center.

下：車両走行試験装置。小牧研究施設
bottom: Rolling Stock Field Test Simulator. Komaki Research Center.

ボンネット下部に補助灯を点灯して試験走行を行うN700系。名古屋駅　2006.4.24
Series N700 test run with supplemental lamps located below the bonnet. Nagoya Station.

浜松駅を通過するN700系。
300系デビューから幕を開けた時速270km運転時代は
700系を経てN700系に引き継がれた。2008.7.29
Series N700 passing through Hamamatsu Station.
The 270 km/h era, which started with the Series 300,
has been overtaken by the Series N700,
which followed the Series 700.

風薫る青空の下、JRセントラルタワーズに見送られて
名古屋駅を発車するN700系。2010.5.17
Series N700 departing Nagoya Station with JR Central Towers
in the background under a beautiful blue sky.

咲き乱れるコスモスを見ながら。米原〜京都間　2008.10.26
Passing through a field of wildly blooming cosmos. Between Maibara and Kyoto.

夕闇を切り裂くエアロ・ダブルウイング。静岡〜掛川間　2013.2
Aero Double Wing cutting through the dim light of the setting sun. Between Shizuoka and Kakegawa.

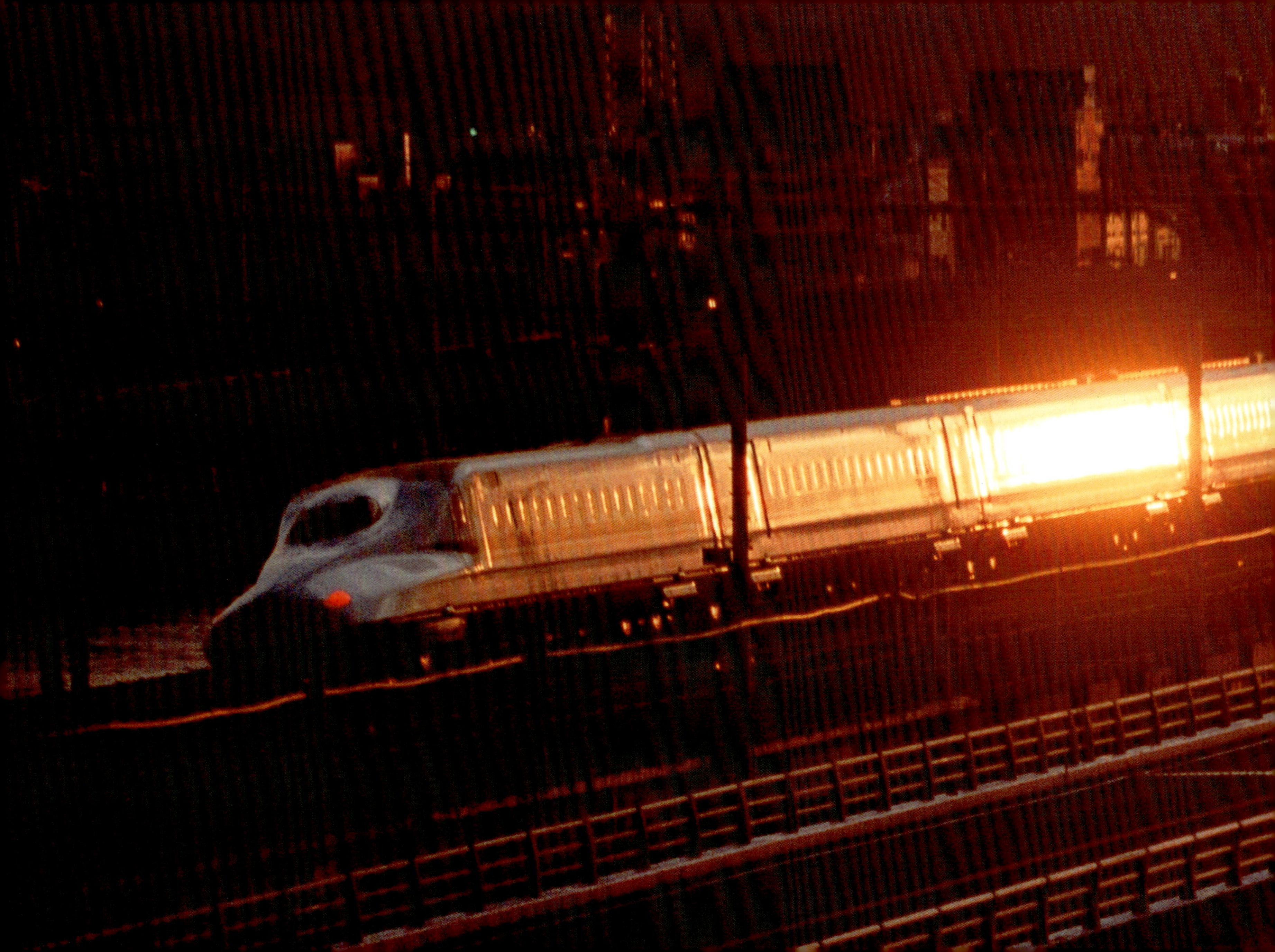

燃えるような浜名湖の夕陽に車体を輝かせて。2009.8.19
top: The trains glow in the reflected light of the sun setting on Lake Hamana.

上：N700系量産先行試作車の運転台。2006.1.11
top: Controls in a Series N700 pre-mass-production trainset.

下：N700系品川始発「のぞみ99号」出発式。品川駅　2007.7.1
bottom: Departure ceremony of Series N700 Nozomi 99 originating from Shinagawa. Shinagawa Station.

日本の大動脈、現在の東海道新幹線の安全安定輸送を担う車両群。
大井基地　2012.12.8
Four Shinkansen representing the current line of safe,
stable transportation on the Tokaido line (Japan's main artery).
Oi Depot.

富士川を渡るN700系。三島〜新富士間　2009.02.12
Series N700 crossing over Fuji River. Between Mishima and Shin-Fuji.

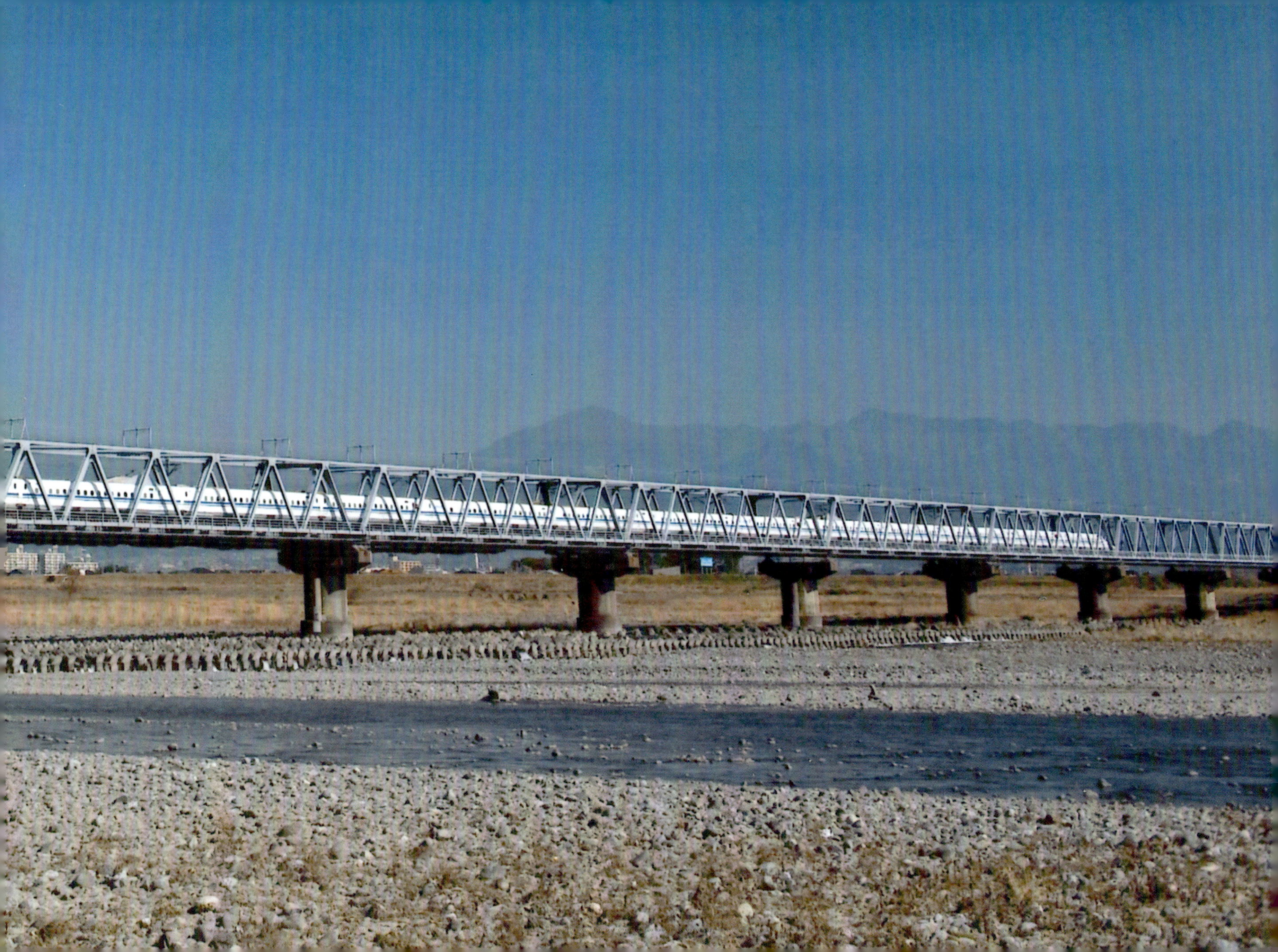

古都京都を行く。2008.12.1
Passing through the old capital of Kyoto.

浜松駅を通過するN700系。車体傾斜装置により、カーブでもスムースで快適な乗り心地を実現した。浜松駅 - 2012.2.24
Series N700 passing Hamamatsu Station. The body inclining system guarantees
a comfortable ride is guaranteed even on curves. Hamamatsu Station.

有楽町駅付近を行く最新型のN700A。2012.9.15
Newest N700A passing through Yurakucho Station.

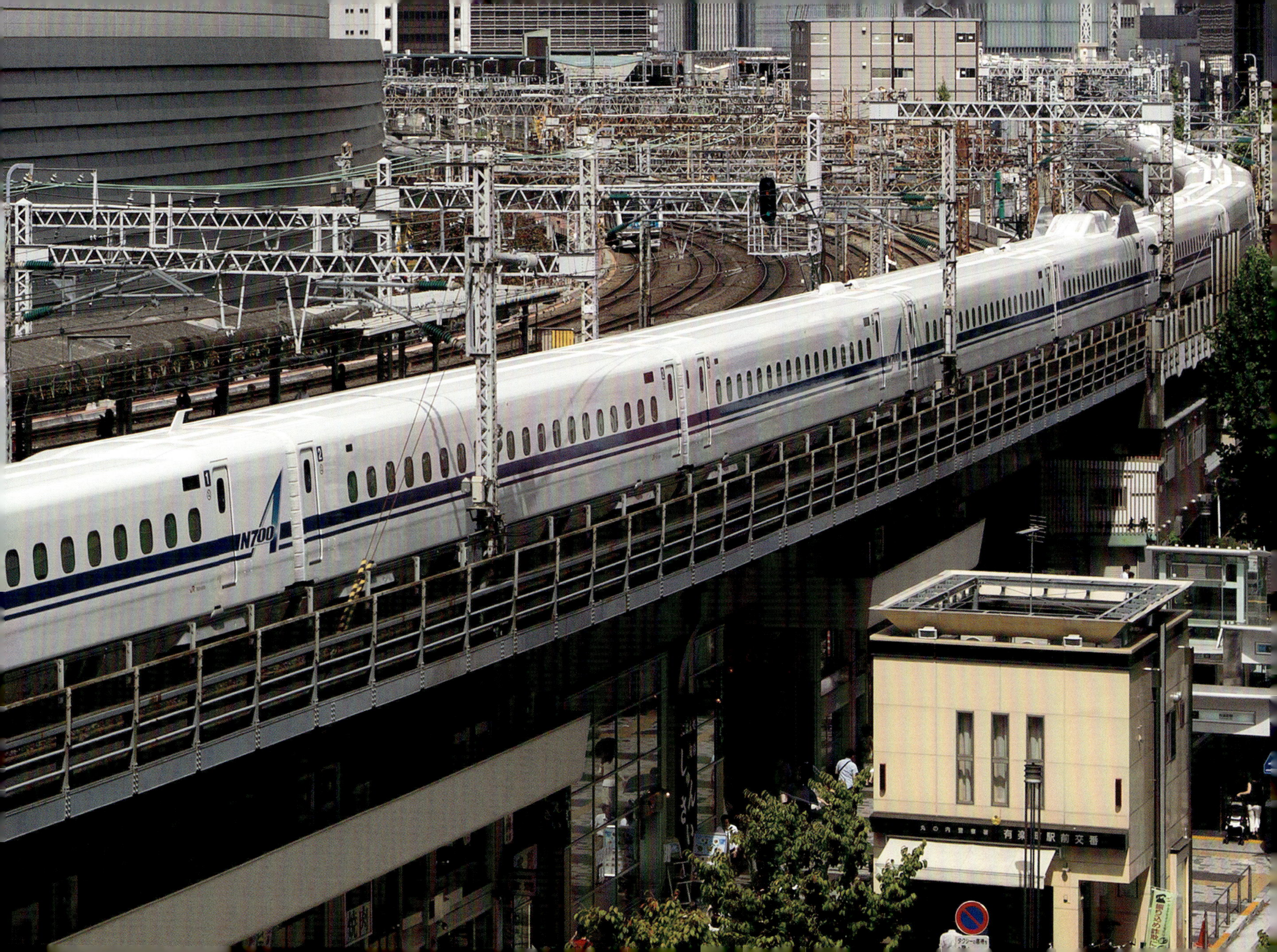
N700
丸の内警察署
有楽町駅前交番

東京駅第9ホーム18、19番線大阪方に設置された第4代国鉄総裁十河信二のレリーフ。「新幹線の父」は今も東海道新幹線を見守っている。2014.4.28
Relief plaque of Shinji Sogo, the fourth JNR president, located on the No. 9 Osaka-bound platform between tracks 18 and 19 in Tokyo Station. Even now the father of the Shinkansen watches over the Tokaido Shinkansen.

153

東海道新幹線開業50周年公式写真集　1964▶2014
ウェッジ編　2014年7月31日　第1刷発行

写真協力 ─────── 広田尚敬
pp.11, 28, 29, 32-34, 35上, 35下左, 35下中, 39左,
41, 60-61, 78 (3), 78 (4), 80 (1).

広田泉
pp. 109, 141

公益財団法人鉄道総合技術研究所
pp. 6-10, 12-14, 17, 22, 23, 24下

鉄道友の会 [久保敏、関崇博、大庭幸雄]
pp.15, 16, 18, 19, 20, 21, 24上, 27, 30-31, 44-51, 53上,
56, 68, 78 (1), 78 (2), 78 (5), 78 (6), 79下, 82 (1-3),
82 (5), 82 (6), 82 (8-10), 82 (12), 82 (13)

毎日新聞社
pp. 26 (1), 26 (2), 79上

読売新聞社
pp. 26 (3), 26 (4)

株式会社交通新聞社
p. 251

東海旅客鉄道株式会社
pp. 35下右, 36-38, 39上, 40, 42-43, 52, 53下, 54, 55,
57-59, 62-63, 64-65, 66, 67, 69-77, 81 (3), 82 (4), 82 (7),
82 (11), 82 (14), 83-85, 86-87, 88-89, 90, 91-97, 98-99,
100-108, 110-111, 112-113, 114-121, 122-123, 124-140,
142-143, 144, 145, 146-147, 148, 149, 150-151, 152-153

株式会社ジェイアール東海パッセンジャーズ
pp. 80 (2-4), 81 (1), 81 (2)

監修 ─────── 須田　寛
副島廣海
田中宏昌

協力 ─────── 東海旅客鉄道株式会社

企画・構成 ─────── 吉村伸一（ウェッジ）
編集 ─────── 根岸あかね（ウェッジ）
翻訳 ─────── フィリップ・ブレイザー
装丁・デザイン ─────── 松村美由起
画像調整・
撮影(p.2,152-153) ─────── ノアーズグラフィック

発行者 ─────── 布施知章
発行所 ─────── 株式会社ウェッジ
〒101-0052
東京都千代田区神田小川町1-3-1
NBF小川町ビルディング3F

電話　03-5280-0528
FAX　03-5217-2661
http://www.wedge.co.jp/
振替　00160-2-410636

印刷・製本所 ─────── 大日本印刷株式会社

©WEDGE Inc. 2014 Printed in Japan
ISBN：978-4-86310-127-2 C0072

定価は本体裏表紙に表示してあります。本書の無断転載を禁じます。
本書の無断複写は著作権法上での例外を除き禁止されています。
本書のいかなる電子複製も購入者の私的使用を除き一切認められておりません。
乱丁本・落丁本は小社にてお取り替えします。
但し古書店等で購入・入手されたものについてはお取り替えできません。

The Official Photo Album to Commemorate the 50th Anniversary of Tokaido Shinkansen

Edited by WEDGE   July 31, 2014, first printing

Photos — Naotaka Hirota
pp.11, 28, 29, 32-34, 35 top, 35 bottom left,
35 bottom center, 39 left, 41, 60-61, 78 (3), 78 (4), 80 (1).

Izumi Hirota
pp. 109, 141

Railway Technical Research Institute
pp. 6-10, 12-14, 17, 22, 23, 24 bottom.

Japan Railfan Club
[Satoshi Kubo, Takahiro Seki, Yukio Oba]
pp.15, 16, 18, 19, 20, 21, 24 top, 27, 30-31, 44-51,
53 top, 56, 68, 78(1), 78(2), 78(5), 78(6), 79 bottom,
82(1-3), 82(5), 82(6), 82(8-10), 82(12), 82(13).

The Mainichi Newspapers
pp. 26(1), 26(2), 79 top.

The Yomiuri Shimbun
pp. 26(3), 26(4).

Transportation News Co., Ltd.
p. 25

Central Japan Railway Company
pp. 35 bottom right, 36-38, 39 top, 40, 42-43, 52,
53 bottom, 54, 55, 57-59, 62-63, 64-65, 66, 67,
69-77, 81(3), 82(4), 82(7), 82(11), 82(14), 83-85,
86-87, 88-89, 90, 91-97, 98-99, 100-108, 110-111,
112-113, 114-121, 122-123, 124-140, 142-143,
144, 145, 146-147, 148, 149, 150-151, 152-153.

JR Central Passengers Co., Ltd.
pp. 80(2-4), 81(1), 81(2).

Supervision — Hiroshi Suda
Hiroumi Soejima
Hiromasa Tanaka

Cooperation — Central Japan Railway Company

Production — Shinichi Yoshimura (WEDGE Inc.)
Editor — Akane Negishi (WEDGE Inc.)
Translation — Philip Brasor
Binding & Design — Miyuki Matsumura
Retouching/
photography (pp. 2, 152-153) — NorsGraphic

Publisher — Tomoaki Fuse
Publishing Co. — WEDGE Inc.
NBF Ogawa-machi Bldg. 3F,
1-3-1 Kanda Ogawa-machi, Chiyoda-ku,
Tokyo 101-0052

Tel. 03-5280-0528
Fax 03-5217-2661
http://www.wedge.co.jp/
Post Office remittance 00160-2-410636

Printing & Binding — Dai Nippon Printing Co., Ltd.

WEDGE Inc. 2014 Printed in Japan
ISBN: 978-4-86310-127-2 C0072

Price is indicated on the back cover.
It is forbidden to reproduce any part of this book in any form without written permission
from the publisher, unless otherwise allowed by copyright law.
It is not permitted to reproduce any content electronically except for private use by the purchaser.
The publisher will exchange any copy that has a manufacturing defect,
except for volumes that were bought second-hand.